GRANDPARENTS OF THE BIBLE
OFFER WISDOM FOR TODAY

GREAT
LESSONS
and
GRAND
BLESSINGS

Discover How Grandparents Can Inspire
and Transform Their Grandchildren

ELMER L. TOWNS

(E) elmertowns

visit us online at elmertowns.com

Great Lessons and Grand Blessings
by Elmer L. Towns

ISBN 13 TP: 978-0-7684-1432-5
ISBN 13 HC: 978-0-7684-1431-8

Original 13 digit ISBN:
978-0-9966734-0-2

Printed in the U.S.A.

Ebook ISBN: 978-0-9966734-1-9

Cover and Interior Design by
Rob Williams, InsideOut Creative Arts
insideoutcreativearts.com

Contents

INTRODUCTION

Being a Grandparent Is Grand

The grandest thing about being a grandparent is the grandchildren. You get to see the miracle of birth a second time around, and all the things you did "wrong" with your first children, you get to do it differently, and hopefully better, the second time with grandchildren.

Being a grandparent means you are older. . . wiser. . . and have seen more. You've experienced more, and accomplished more. Now in your "grand" years, you get to influence your grandchildren.

Giving the best of your life,
For the rest of your life,
Because your grandchildren become
The test of your life.

Because you've experienced more in life, you have a big picture. You see more potential in your grandchildren than anyone else. So do everything possible to show them their potential and that they reach their potential.

Because you've experienced both failure and success, you know there's not a lot of distance between them. So you'll have to help your grandchildren overcome their problems and troubles, and their fears and failures. You'll have to help them forget their disappointments. Then, you'll have to applaud their successes, because you know a successful life is sculpted out of the experiences we do best.

Because we (Ruth and Elmer) are grandparents of ten, we've learned a little along the way about child rearing. We don't claim to be perfect parents/grandparents—if we were, our offspring would be perfect—we just praise the Lord for the grand opportunity to be parents again by being grandparents.

What a terrible thing to race through strife,

Running to win first place in life,

And when you get there, no one applauds your run,

So God created grandparents to say, "Well done."

Along the way, Elmer and I have learned a few lessons. We've tried to pass them on to our grandchildren and others by our teaching. A few of the things we've learned have been written in this book, so you can become better parents/grandparents as you read these biblical models. But remember, your parental skills will not be measured by how well you master this book, but by how well you influence your children, grandchildren, and great-grandchildren.

Changed lives for God, that's the purpose of this book.

Ruth was adopted, so she really liked the chapter on Mordecai's adopting Esther and influencing her to become the Queen of Persia, the greatest nation on the earth at that time. Elmer's father was an alcoholic and the grandfathers on both sides of the family were hard-liquor drinking men, so he liked the chapter on Asa and Josiah, boys who overcame detrimental family influences to live for God and serve Him.

What will be your favorite chapter? Probably the one that helps you become a better grandparent. Our purpose is that these stories will change your life.

Our prayer: May God give us better grandparents so that the world may be a better place.

Sincerely yours in Christ,
Elmer L.Towns

Written from our home at the foot of
the Blue Ridge Mountains of Virginia

1

Jacob:

Grandfather of Ephraim and Manassah

A Grandfather Blesses His Grandchildren

GRANDFATHER—JACOB
FATHER—JOSEPH
GRANDSONS—MANASSEH AND EPHRAIM

"Then Israel stretched out his right hand and laid it on Ephraim's head, who was the younger, and his left hand on Manasseh's head, guiding his hands knowingly, for Manasseh was the firstborn. . . The Angel who has redeemed me from all evil, Bless the lads; Let my name be named upon them, the name of my fathers Abraham and Isaac; And let them grow into a multitude in the midst of the earth. Now when Joseph saw that his father laid his right hand on the head of Ephraim, it displeased him; so he took hold of his father's hand to remove it from Ephraim's head to Manasseh's head. And Joseph said to his father, 'Not so, my father, for this one is the firstborn; put your right hand on his head.' But his father refused and said, 'I know, my son, I know. He also shall become a people, and he also shall be great; but truly his younger brother shall be greater than he, and his descendants shall become a multitude of nations.'"

GENESIS 48:14, 16-19

The footsteps echoed off the white marbled walls of the palace; young Ephraim was running through the halls to his brother's bedroom. Ephraim was the youngest son of Joseph, who was the minister of agriculture in Egypt, second to Pharaoh. His black flashing eyes reflected his father Joseph, a Hebrew; his fair skin reflected his mother, an Egyptian. Because of his father's wealth, servants were stationed everywhere throughout his palace and both boys had a private attendant.

"Manasseh," the younger boy yelled out the name of his older and larger brother, "Guess where we're going today?" His excited yell turned the servants' heads. Ephraim burst into his brother's bedroom to announce, "We're going to see Grandpa Jacob today."

Ephraim was barely winded. He was the more athletic of the two boys, also the more daring, the more aggressive and, when it came to curiosity, Ephraim was the one who always got into trouble. Joseph felt that Ephraim was more like his Grandfather Jacob than any of his 12 sons.

Ephraim and Manasseh huddled with excitement to leave the boring city and travel to Grandpa Jacob's farm country in the Nile Delta where everything was green, lush and there were sheep and cows everywhere. In the city where the boys lived, white stone buildings rose from the white surrounding sand. Everything was dry . . . hot . . . arid.

Grandpa Jacob always told stories of traveling to the far nation of Mesopotamia and being a shepherd and sleeping on the ground, under the stars. His tales of killing wild predators thrilled the boys, as well as his stories about fighting and taking the city Shechem and Mount Gerizim. The boys' other grandfather, Potipherah, priest of On, worshipped the Egyptian god Re. When their mother Asenaph took them to visit her father, Grandpa Potipherah, he tried to teach them the Egyptian name of the different stars and how to worship the stars.

But the boys believed in Grandpa Jacob's God, not Grandpa Potipherah's god.

As the chariot rumbled through the burning sands of the Egyptian Desert, they saw camels—the desert travelers. As they got closer to Grandpa Jacob's home, the landscape slowly changed to the green pastures of the Nile Delta where they saw sheep and cattle grazing in green fields.

A rank of soldiers headed the procession; they went everywhere with Joseph, not so much for protection, but as a statement of prestige. Behind the boys came servants and other Egyptian dignitaries.

Grandpa Jacob knew the boys were coming, so he had forced himself to get dressed, slipping into his comfortable shepherd's tunic faded with age, rumpled and worn. Like most old people, Jacob didn't pay attention to his clothes for he didn't see well, and style doesn't matter when you're ready to die. The coat had the smell of sheep and perspiration, but old people don't smell as well as when they were younger; Jacob wore clothes that were comfortable.

Joseph greeted his father warmly, as he had always done. Egyptian scribes were along to record the events, for the last words of great men were important for posterity.

Joseph had brought the best doctors available in the palace. They knew the latest cures and could mix many herbs and potions. But old Jacob shook his head no to the doctor; he relied on the techniques he had learned in the field, shepherding his sheep.

Jacob took control of the meeting, telling everyone, "When I was a young man running away from home, God Almighty appeared to me in a mountain named Bethel—it means the 'House of God'—and I needed reassurance from the LORD. My brother Esau wanted to kill me. That night God appeared to me in a dream saying, *'Behold, I the Lord will prosper you in all that you do, I will give you many children, and you will become a great nation. I the Lord promise this land to you—a promised land—that you shall inherit this land for an everlasting possession.'"*

Then Jacob told the part of the story that hurt. He told how his sons hated Joseph and tried to kill Joseph, but sold him into slavery. In slavery, God protected Joseph and elevated him to rule over all the agriculture of Egypt.

Then Grandfather Jacob abruptly asked, "Are these your two sons—Ephraim and Manasseh—who were born to you in the land of Egypt before I came here?"

Then Jacob made the pronouncement that the two grandsons would be adopted by him. Even though Ephraim and Manasseh were half Egyptian, old Jacob wanted everyone to know that these two boys would have a Hebrew inheritance, so he announced before all, "These boys are mine." Then he turned to the Scribes, noting, "Write it down, just as I said."

To make sure that they all understood, Jacob continued, "These two boys are mine, just as much as Reuben and Simeon are mine."

Again, Jacob turned to the Scribes noting, "These shall be placed in order after their brethren in my inheritance."

Even though Joseph was one of the richest men in Egypt, and Joseph could give his sons more wealth than Jacob ever conceived, it was important for the old man to give the boys something. Jacob's inheritance was important because every one of his sheep and cattle were given by God. When a few things are all that the man has, these few things are important to him and to his grandsons. And in giving to his grandsons what he had, Jacob was giving them his identity, his character and his life.

"Bring your sons to me," Jacob said, pointing to Ephraim and Manasseh. The situation that followed was filled with tension, for Joseph knew what should be done, but wily old Jacob knew what he would do.

Joseph brought the boys to his father, according to their birth order. Jacob's left hand was to be on the head of younger Ephraim, his second born. Jacob's right hand—the hand of authority—was to be on the head of Manasseh, his first born. Then Joseph bowed his head. As the boys approached, Jacob crossed his arms, placing his right hand on the head of Ephraim who was the younger and his left hand to Manasseh, the older. The old grandfather blessed his grandsons.

"Lord, You redeemed me from the Evil One, now Lord, protect these young boys from evil. Let my name be on them, and let my inheritance be their inheritance. May the names of Abraham, Isaac and Jacob be upon these boys and may they grow into a multitude on the earth."

When Joseph looked up, he saw that Jacob's right hand was on Ephraim, the younger son. He objected, saying, "Not so, father, you have your hand of blessing on Ephraim, but he is the second born."

Jacob didn't respond, but smiled inwardly, knowing he was doing God's will. He told Joseph, "Remember God's principle of choice. When I was born second, the Lord told my mother that the *older shall serve the younger*, meaning the second born will rule the first born." That day Jacob gave Ephraim the spiritual birthright, which included the spiritual leadership of the family clan, as well as the right to pray for all the family.

Jacob could not have known what would happen to Ephraim, but God knew. One day the entire nation of Israel would be called by the name *Ephraim*, and one day the tribe of Ephraim would have more people than any other tribe, and more soldiers than any of the other twelve tribes of Israel. The prosperity of the tribe of Ephraim would flow into all of the other eleven tribes, making each of them wealthy.

But not to leave Manasseh out, Jacob explained to Joseph, "Manasseh will be a great people, he will become a great nation, but his young brother Ephraim will be a greater people and the children of Ephraim shall lead the children of Manasseh."

"Write what I have said," Jacob again turned to the scribes and said, and they did.

"Behold, I die!" Grandpa Jacob told everyone in the room.

When Jacob used the word *death,* no one knew whether he meant minutes…hours…days…or even years. But somehow in their hearts, they knew death was imminent. Jacob added a final blessing for all his family, "God will be with you, and bring the nation out of Egypt back in to the Promised Land; because God promised, He will take you back to the land of our fathers."

What Can a Grandfather Do?

Lesson to Take Away
When grandparents can't spend much time with their grandchildren, or give them much material inheritance, their greatest gift can be to spiritually bless and pray for their grandchildren.

What could Grandpa Jacob give his grandchildren? He was poor in worldly goods compared to their wealthy father Joseph. They lived in a palace, had access to the best universities of Egypt, had household servants, and all of the symbols of power. Grandfather Jacob had nothing to give his grandchildren but the *blessing* that God gave him.

Jacob was an absentee grandfather that his grandchildren seldom saw? The children of Joseph lived in the city where Joseph was minister of agriculture for Egypt. Grandpa Jacob lived far removed in the Nile delta, in rural conditions; a completely different way of life. When a grandfather doesn't see his grandsons very often, he can give them a *spiritual inheritance* because God is everywhere and he can transcend boundaries to touch the lives of his grandchildren.

What could physically weak Jacob do for his grandchildren? When a grandfather can no longer walk down a trail with his grandchildren, nor is he physically able to sit and talk with his grandchildren, when they come for a visit, what can he do? A grandfather can put *his name* upon them, as well as the *name of the Lord,* Who will always be with the grandchildren.

What can a grandfather give to his grandchildren when he has nothing left to give? The most important thing that you can give to your grandchildren is not money, possessions, or even the homestead. The most important thing is a *spiritual heritage* to guide their life.

Four Things Grandpa Jacob Said to Them

1. Grandpa Jacob gave his testimony to his grandsons. When the boys finally arrived at Jacob's home, and he was ready for an important audience with them, Jacob gave the boys his testimony. Had the boys heard the testimony before? Did they know it by heart? That's not the issue. Jacob thought it was important to *rehearse* for them what God had done for him. Grandpa Jacob began, "God Almighty appeared to me at Luz in the land of Canaan and blessed me" (Gen. 48:3). Was Grandpa Jacob sharing his salvation experience? Was Grandpa Jacob just telling his grandsons about a life-changing experience? Jacob told the boys how he met God at Bethel.

What Happened When God Met Jacob at Bethel

"Now Jacob went out from Beersheba and went toward Haran. So he came to a certain place and stayed there all night, because the sun had set. And he took one of the stones of that place and put it at his head, and he lay down in that place to sleep. Then he dreamed, and behold, a ladder was set up on the earth, and its top reached to heaven; and there the angels of God were ascending and descending on it. And behold, the LORD stood above it and said: I am the LORD God of Abraham your father and the God of Isaac; the land on which you lie I will give to you and your descendants. Also your descendants shall be as the dust of the earth;

you shall spread abroad to the west and the east, to the north and the south; and in you and in your seed all the families of the earth shall be blessed. Behold, I am with you and will keep you wherever you go, and will bring you back to this land; for I will not leave you until I have done what I have spoken to you. Then Jacob awoke from his sleep and said, Surely the LORD *is in this place, and I did not know it. And he was afraid and said, How awesome is this place! This is none other than the house of God, and this is the gate of heaven! Then Jacob rose early in the morning, and took the stone that he had put at his head, set it up as a pillar, and poured oil on top of it. And he called the name of that place Bethel; but the name of that city had been Luz previously. Then Jacob made a vow, saying, If God will be with me, and keep me in this way that I am going, and give me bread to eat and clothing to put on, so that I come back to my father's house in peace, then the* LORD *shall be my God. And this stone which I have set as a pillar shall be God's house, and of all that You give me I will surely give a tenth to You" (Gen. 28:10-22).*

Grandfathers like to tell stories over and over, just as much as grandchildren like to hear them repeatedly. When Manassas and Ephraim visited their grandfather—perhaps for the last time—Jacob thought that it was important to tell the boys about his encounter with God. "God, before whom my fathers Abraham and Isaac walked, the God who has fed me all my life long to this day" (Gen. 48:15).

What's Involved in Giving Your Testimony?

1. What you were before salvation.
2. What you did to receive Christ.
3. How you were changed.

2. Jacob told the boys about God. Jacob reminded them that God's name was "God Almighty" (v. 3). Today there is power in the name of Jesus, as well as healing in Jesus' name, deliverance in Jesus' name, and answered prayer in Jesus' name (Acts 3:6; 4:12; 5:28; John 14:13, 14). Tell your grandchildren what the name of Jesus means to you.

Today grandparents can tell their grandchildren stories from the Bible, but Jacob didn't have a Bible. He had to quote from memory what God said.

Jacob shared with his grandsons what God expected him to do. You must tell your grandchildren that God expects them to believe in Him, live for Him, and to grow as a Christian. In a real sense, today you must challenge your grandchildren to believe in Christ for salvation, live by the Word of God, and prepare themselves for Heaven.

3. Grandpa Jacob told them the fourfold promise of God. Jacob reminded the young boys of God's promise to him. Much of the original promises of God to Abraham were repeated to Jacob. Jacob was the one through whom the blessing of God would come.

"Behold, I the Lord will prosper you in all that
you do, I will give you many children, and you will
become a great nation. I the Lord promise this land
to you—a promised land—that you shall inherit
this land for an everlasting possession"
(adapted from Gen. 48:4).

---

4. Grandpa Jacob told them about their grandmother. Since grandmother Rachel was not present when Jacob passed the birthright on to the next generation, Grandpa Jacob had to remind his grandsons about her. He said, "When I came from Padan, Rachel died beside me in the land of Canaan on the way, when there was but a little distance to go to Ephrath; and I buried her there" (Gen. 48:7).

It's important that both grandfather and grandmother include the other when blessing their grandchildren. The love and care that grandparents have for each other should extend to grandchildren. And not just love, but also their combined wisdom, prayers, financial and spiritual inheritance.

What Jacob Said About Their Grandmother

1. Your grandmother died in travel.
2. I was there when she died.
3. We were almost home.
4. She was buried by the road.

Four Things Grandpa Jacob Did for Them

When it came to blessing the children, Jacob said many things to them; but words sometimes are not enough. There must be deeds to backup your words. So grandpa Jacob did four things for his grandsons.

1. Grandpa Jacob adopted them. When Jacob asked to see the boys, he made a very bold statement. The boys were half Hebrew and half Egyptian, but Jacob looked beyond their Egyptian nature he wanted the boys to have the spiritual inheritance of Israel. So Jacob said, "And now your two sons, Ephraim and Manasseh . . . are mine" (Gen. 48:5). This would have been astonishing to those who heard Jacob, for this was the language of adoption. Many families would have put a full-blooded Hebrew child far beyond a half-breed youth. But not Jacob. The love of Jacob in his heart for these two boys transcended normal tribal prejudice. He made a legal pronouncement to adopt Ephraim and Manasseh.

2. Grandpa Jacob kissed and hugged them. It was important in the Jewish economy to show affection to the children. But a blessing was more than showing affection; it was reflected in Jacob's heart overflowing for these boys to carry out his inheritance. "He kissed and embraced them" (Gen. 48:10).

When blessing a grandchild, you must do more than just say words over them. You pour your soul into them, and how do you do that? Your soul is transferred by the love you show them. When you kiss a child, embrace a child, and let him know that you love him, you're doing more than an outward physical symbol. You're putting your life into their life. This is similar to what Paul said to the Thessalonians: "You received not just the Word of God from us, but it was the Word of God in our hearts that was poured into your life, effectually making you what you are in Christ" (1 Thess. 2:13, author's translation).

3. Grandpa Jacob laid his hands on them. The blessing of grandparents must be transferred to their grandchildren; but how can it be done? Remember, God likes symbols. He loves the symbol in the Lord's Table of the broken body and the spilt blood, just as He loves the symbols of the cross and the symbol of steeples that symbolically point the way to God. So when you bless a child, place your hands on his or her head, symbolizing your approval of the child, as well as a picture of your life flowing into theirs: "Then Israel stretched out his right hand and laid it on Ephraim's head, who was the younger, and his left hand on Manasseh's head, guiding his hands knowingly, for Manasseh was the firstborn" (Gen. 48:14). Jacob knew what he was doing: he was following the law that God had applied in his own life, i.e., *the oldest shall serve the youngest.* Jacob was blessing Ephraim—the second born—with the birthright of the family. Jacob was giving Ephraim the responsibility of spiritual leadership and intercession for the family. Even though Joseph protested, Jacob was led of God to bless Ephraim. Why? Because God saw that the future children of Ephraim would be leaders among the twelve tribes of Israel.

4. Grandpa Jacob blessed his grandchildren. The New Testament Hall of Fame says, "By faith Jacob, when he was dying, blessed each of the sons of Joseph" (Heb. 11:21). At that time, there was no Levitical blessing to give to the sons; however, when a grandparent today is blessing his grandchild, he can use the Levitical blessing.

The Levitical Blessing

"The Lord bless you and keep you; The Lord make His face shine upon you, and be gracious to you; The Lord lift up His countenance upon you, and give you peace" (Num. 6:24-26).

It's important for grandparents to bless their grandchildren. This is done in different ways, at different times, and for different purposes. Do it with boldness; however, some grandparents do it reluctantly. If the grandparent is reticent, children are sensitive; they will recognize their fearfulness, and the blessing may lose its meaning.

What should you do to bless your grandchildren? The following outline may give you some insight: (1) Pray and ask God to prepare you and help you. (2) Pray and ask God to prepare your grandchildren to receive the blessing. (3) Pray and ask God to give you the words to pray. (4) Find a meaningful reference in your Bible, highlight it for them to see, and/or write the reference on a separate sheet of paper. Be ready to share Bible verses with your grandchildren. (5) Do more than bless spiritually; make sure your grandchildren know what you plan to do for them in support of God's will for their life, how you will plan for them materially, and what you will do for them financially. (6) Make sure that you place special value on your grandchildren long before the actual event of blessing them, and long after you have blessed them. Your placing hands on their head is not enough; your lifestyle must be a blessing to them. A blessing is *both* a long-term attitude of blessing as well as a singular event of blessing. (7) Grandparents must not just wait for the grandchild to carry out the blessing in their life; a grandparent must make an active commitment to fulfill the blessing in the life of their grandchildren in every way possible. Grandparents must give their grandchildren time, counsel, example, and money.

How to Bless Children

1. A meaningful touch.
2. Blessing with a spoken word.
3. Attach high value to the one being blessed.
4. Picture of special future for the one being blessed.
5. An active commitment to fulfill the blessing
   (From *God Bless You*, Elmer Towns, Regal Books, 2003)

Four Things Grandpa Jacob Gave Them

This could have been an embarrassing situation. Jacob didn't have money or material resources to give to the grandsons, as did their father Joseph. Jacob didn't have time or strength; he had nothing to give but the blessing of God. So what did Grandpa Jacob give to them?

1. Grandpa Jacob gave them his name. When Jacob adopted the two boys and brought them into the family line, he made them a part of his inheritance. Notice what he said, "Let my name be named upon them, and the name of my fathers Abraham and

Isaac" (Gen. 48:16). When Jacob said before everyone, "They are mine" (Gen. 48:5), the boys legally became a part of his family.

It's important that your grandchildren know they belong to you, that they have a special connection to you. You are not their parents, so you cannot do everything that their parents do. Nor are you an aunt or an uncle. You are their grandparent, and you have a grandparent's responsibility. What is that responsibility?

(1) You must accept them fully, without hesitation or qualification. (2) You must recognize that they have your blood flowing in their veins. (3) You must recognize that none of your grandchildren are second-class family members. (4) You must love each equally, apart from time and circumstances. (5) You must give yourself to them as time and circumstances permit.

2. Grandpa Jacob gave God's future to them. God is the greatest thing that you can give to a child. You have given them the greatest thing in life when you give them knowledge of the Lord, and access to the Lord, and the promises of the Lord, and a vision of the Lord.

Jacob told his grandsons about the future. He said, "let them grow into a multitude in the midst of the earth" (Gen. 48:16). And then Jacob gave them the following, "So he blessed them that day, saying, 'By you Israel will bless . . .' And thus he set Ephraim before Manasseh" (Gen. 48:20).

3. Grandpa Jacob gave them his love. When you give a child your love, it's much more than giving a hug and a kiss. Love is opening up your heart to give yourself to the one you love. Isn't that what God did for us? "He loved us and sent His Son to be the propitiation for our sins" (1 John 4:10). There was nothing more that God could give to us than His Son, and there's nothing more that you can share with your grandchildren than God's Son.

4. Grandpa Jacob gave them an example of worship. Apparently Jacob was sitting on a bed, i.e., an Egyptian bed. This was probably not a bed raised off the floor like Americans sleep in. Jacob's bed was probably lying on a heavy blanket on the floor, similar to our spreading out a sleeping bag on the floor.

Jacob worshipped in two ways. First, "He bowed down with his face to the earth" (Gen. 48:12). He didn't have to get out of bed. He just got up on his elbows and knees to worship. Jacob thanked God for the opportunity of passing his spiritual inheritance on to his children. Then Jacob must have propped himself up, using his shepherd's staff for support. As he leaned on his staff, Jacob blessed his grandchildren.

   a. Jacob's position of worship. Even though many were watching Jacob, he was more concerned with God than with what people thought. "He bowed down with his face to the earth" (Gen. 48:12). When one prostrates oneself before God, it's because God is everything, and we offer ourselves to Him in service. This was Jacob's heart position.

   b. Jacob's attitude of blessing. The Christian Hall of Fame describes, "When he was dying . . . leaning upon the top of his staff" (Heb. 11:21). Jacob must have propped himself up with his shepherd's staff, as he blessed the boys. Because of his advanced age, he might not have been able to support himself on his knees, so he propped himself on his staff.

Lessons to Take Away

1. Grandparents should be concerned about the spiritual condition of their grandchildren. Jacob didn't let pressure divert him away from his main goal, i.e., imparting spiritual blessing to his grandchildren. Every grandparent must have such a deep commitment to God that they will not let anything get in their way of communicating their faith to their grandchildren. Your passion is more important than any technique you use to influence them. Your heart is more important than any method you use, such as a phone call, a note, or cooking them a meal. Grandparents should be deeply concerned about the spiritual condition of their grandchildren.

   2. Grandparents should be spiritual examples. What image do your grandchildren have of you? What do they think, and what do they remember? Sometimes words are forgotten, but good deeds that bless the children are always remembered. Therefore be a great example to your grandchildren.

We (Ruth and Elmer) have been teaching in Christian colleges for almost fifty years. Over the years, we've noted a great change in the attitude toward the grandparents of young people who come to Christian colleges. During the 1950s to 1970s, we don't remember Christian young people saying a lot about their grandparents. There may have been conditional reasons why young people during that time didn't talk about their grandparents as much. However, in the 1980s and 1990s we noticed the Christian young people often spoke with deep appreciation for their grandparents. Christian young people share prayer requests of their grandparents' physical needs, and taking time off in school to attend grandparents' wedding anniversaries, family reunions, and even going home to visit grandparents when they're in the hospital. Young people didn't seem to be that concerned about their grandparents fifty years ago. What's the difference? As more mothers have gone back to work, the entire family has less time to spend on children. Mothers who work forty hours a week in secular employment still have all their jobs around the house when they come home. As a result, children receive less time from their parents. True, parents today do a lot with their young people in sports teams and different clubs, but parents don't have time to just sit around talking, listening, and counseling. It's the grandparents who have more time than anyone else, they listen better than anyone else, and grandparents can mentor because they understand more about life than anyone else.

Also, grandparents are more forgiving than parents. Why? Because parents are responsible for the discipline and good behavior of their kids; but grandparents can overlook their failures and disobedience, and love them anyway. *Go ahead and eat your dessert before dinner. Want another cookie?*

3. Grandparents should give their testimony. One of the best ways to make sure your grandchildren live for God is to tell them how you did it. When you share your victories and defeats, grandchildren will listen, and remember. They like stories, so tell them your life story. Tell them how you came to know Christ, how your life was changed, and what God has done for you through all of your years. Do you know the greatest answer to prayer you've ever had? Yes, you probably know; but do your grandchildren know? What's the greatest insight you've gotten from the Bible? Who's the greatest way God has used you in Christian ministry? What's the greatest Christian friend you've ever had? You know these things, but do your grandchildren? They won't unless you tell them.

4. Grandparents should bless their grandchildren both naturally and supernaturally. There are so many ways that grandparents can bless naturally, e.g., by taking them for a hamburger, going to the amusement park, or coaching them about life skills, such as woodworking, hobbies, cooking, repairing an engine, or the vast other skills that grandparents have learned in their lifetime. Pass that on to your grandchildren naturally, and you bless them naturally.

But don't forget that you bless them spiritually when you coach them concerning the spiritual things you know. You know how to use a concordance to find verses in the Bible, but do your grandchildren? You know how to answer questions about the existence of God. What is the will of God? How can they know you're saved? And what attitudes and actions does God not want them to do? You'll bless your grandchildren spiritually when you give them that information.

To bless your grandchildren takes intention. You must plan to bless them. Make an appointment to be with them and bless them. Be intentional in carrying out the blessing. Why? Because there's an enemy who wants the souls of your grandchildren. He will steal the Word of God from their hearts if you let him. He will steal spiritual convictions from their heart if you let him; so plan to bless your grandchildren spiritually.

2

Naomi:

Grandmother of Obed

A Compromising Mother Becomes
An Influential Grandmother

GRANDMOTHER—NAOMI
MOTHER—RUTH
GRANDSON—OBED

*"So Boaz took Ruth and she became his wife; and when he went in to her, the
LORD gave her conception, and she bore a son. Then the women said to Naomi,
'Blessed be the LORD, who has not left you this day without a close relative; and
may his name be famous in Israel! And may he be to you a restorer of life and a
nourisher of your old age; for your daughter-in-law, who loves you, who is better
to you than seven sons, has borne him.' Then Naomi took the child and laid him
on her bosom, and became a nurse to him. Also the neighbor women gave him a
name, saying, 'There is a son born to Naomi.' And they called his name Obed.
He is the father of Jesse, the father of David."*

RUTH 4:13-17

The little boy stopped at the back door to smile at his grandmother, Naomi. The boy had been playing in the clay at the back wash table. He had made walls—like the walls of a city—and now his make-believe city was drying in the sun. His little hands were not yet skilled, so the little city was crude.

"Look," he said to his grandmother, "I made a city." And with that, the little boy stepped on the wall and said, "Like God crushed the walls of Jericho." Then the boy asked his grandmother to tell the story again.

Naomi gave little Obed a cup of milk and set him at the table. Then Naomi told how his great-grandmother Rahab had lived in Jericho. She told how Rahab lived on the top of the wall in a small inn. There, travelers stayed the night.

Naomi told young Obed how generations ago God planned to destroy Jericho, but first two of God's servants came to spy out Jericho. They rented rooms in the small inn, and when the spies realized that Rahab and her family trusted in Jehovah, the spies told them what God was going to do. "God will destroy the city of Jericho," the spies told the family. (Rahab was formerly a sinful woman.)

"But we believe in Jehovah," Rahab told the spies. It was then that the two spies told Rahab that if she would hang a long red rope out of her window, she and her family would be saved when the Israeli army attacked Jericho. Grandma Naomi told how the priests marched around Jericho once a day. They carried the Ark of the Covenant—the presence of God—around the city once a day for seven days, and then on the seventh day, they marched around the city seven times.

"KABOOM!" Grandma Naomi made a big noise to tell her young grandson how God brought down the walls of Jericho. Then she reminded, "God saved Rahab and her family."

"Rahab was your other grandmother," Naomi explained to the young kid who seemed to understand.

Rahab married one of God's servants, and they had a child named Boaz. "The little baby Boaz was your father," Grandma Naomi's high pitched voice got young Obed excited.

Then Grandma Naomi began to share her story, telling about a famine that came to Bethlehem. "See these rich grain fields," Grandma Naomi pointed out the door towards Boaz's wheat fields. "Long ago they were dry, nothing would grow, and everything died."

"How did you eat?" the young Obed asked his grandmother.

"We moved to the country of Moab," Naomi took the young boy to the door where she pointed. And miles away across a valley that was far away. "That's Moab." Naomi told how her husband and both of her sons died in Moab. "I thought I also would die in Moab," she told her grandson. "But just before I starved, I decided to come back home to Bethlehem."

Then Naomi's face smiled. She told her young grandson about saying goodbye to everyone she knew in Moab. Everyone left her but Ruth who wanted to come with her to Bethlehem. Naomi explained, "Your mother wanted to come with me because she believed in Jehovah."

"Your mother and I didn't have anything to eat when we got here, so your mother went into the grain fields to pick up any food she could find. She just happened to go to one of your father's fields. When your father and your mother saw each other, it was love at first sight." Naomi told how Boaz flirted with Ruth. Grandma Naomi explained, "Your father invited your mother Ruth to come eat from his food basket, then he told all of the workers to drop grain right in front of your mother. You know what? Your mother got more grain than anybody else that day."

Little Obed laughed. He liked the part about his mother bringing home a whole sack full of grain.

"You were their first baby," Grandma Naomi explained to the little boy, "and I get to take care of you."

"Tell me how I got my name," the little boy begged, "please tell me the story again."

Grandma Naomi told how a baby is named when he is eight days old. "Your father wanted to call him after himself, i.e., Boaz, and your mother had a different name; but all the women at the village said, 'No!!' They wouldn't hear of it. The women said that everybody praised God because you were such a beautiful baby boy that was born to Boaz and Ruth. You were in the line of Messiah." Then Naomi said, "One day Messiah will come through you; he will born of our family." Naomi explained that because the women praised and worshipped God so much, "You were called Obed, which means worship of the Lord."

"But that's not all," the little boy reminded his grandmother.

"Yes," she smiled in agreement with the little boy. "Obed also means servant; you are a servant who will bring worship to the Lord."

How Naomi Compromised

Lesson to Take Away

A parent can do a terrible job raising their children, but the Lord (the God of the second chance) can give them a second opportunity to do it right with grandchildren.

Naomi must have been quite a woman in her day. She and her husband were called "Ephrathites of Bethlehem." A phrase that means they were *bluebloods* or *upper class,* or in our day, "the rich and famous." Technically the term *ephrathites* meant they were the original families of Bethlehem.

Naomi came from Bethlehem, a city that meant *House of Bread,* but after she got married it was anything but a house of bread. Fields turned brown, trees dropped their leaves, and nothing grew. The Bible says, "there was a famine in the land" (Ruth 1:1).

When difficult times come, people of character tighten their belts and with true grit they may get through difficult days. But not Naomi and her husband Elimelech. From Bethlehem you can look miles across the Dead Sea Valley and see Moab in the cloudy distance. They saw the green fields of Moab in stark contrast to the famine around them. Was it greed that motivated them to go to Moab, was it a search for a better life, maybe it was an excuse like many modern families, "I'm doing it for my family who needs the best of everything"?

What Did Naomi Leave?

- She left the land of promise for a land of compromise.
- She left the Temple in Jerusalem for a land of idols.
- She left the fellowship of God's people for unsaved heathen.
- She ran away from her problem, seeking an easy life.

When Naomi and Elimelech went to Moab, at first they just "went to sojourn" (Ruth 1:1), which means they were going to ride out the agricultural storm in Moab. They were probably planning on returning home.

But they didn't return home. Elimelech died in Moab. Was it God's punishment for compromise? Strange, Elimelech went to Moab to keep from dying, but it was there he died. Isn't that like people who don't want to give up anything for the Lord, yet they end up losing what they can't keep because they won't surrender to the Lord? Perhaps the problem is not that they settled down in Moab, but rather Moab settled down in them. The Bible says, "They went to the country of Moab and remained there" (Ruth 1:2). Maybe conditions were easier in Moab, and all they could remember about the Promised Land was famine. Remember, it's not always easy to remain in the center of God's will; sometimes it's extremely difficult to remain in God's presence.

Next, the two sons married heathen women. Mahlon married Orpah, and Chilion married Ruth. The Bible doesn't mention any children, even though they were married for ten years. So without a husband, Naomi remained in Moab for a decade, no purpose, no plans, and no hope. She was waiting for the children that her two sons would give her; but children didn't come. Then Mahlon died and shortly thereafter Chilion died. Now you have three widows—three desperate women—without husbands, without money, and without hope in the future.

Naomi compromised her commitment to the Lord. Naomi decided to return to the Promised Land; what else could she do? It seems her decision was made in desperation, rather than a spiritual commitment to God. Her two daughters-in-law decided to return with her, but Naomi discouraged them. "Go, return each to her mother's house. The Lord deal kindly with you, as you have dealt with the dead and with me" (Ruth 1:8). This seemed to be Naomi's honest desire for the two widows to have a remaining life. But then Naomi makes a tragic blunder.

Orpah started back to her family, but Ruth decided not to go. Ruth decided to stay with Naomi. It's then that Naomi says, "Look, your sister-in-law has gone back to her people and to her gods; return after your sister-in-law" (Ruth 1:15). Naomi wanted Ruth to return to her family and her heathen gods. But Ruth displayed faith in Jehovah. In this tragic moment of choice, Ruth made a decision that revealed her deep faith in God.

"Entreat me not to leave you, or to turn back from following after you; for wherever you go, I will go; and wherever you lodge, I will lodge; your people shall be my people, and your God, my God. Where you die, I will die, and there will I be buried. The Lord do so to me, and more also, if anything but death parts you and me" (Ruth 1:16, 17).

Naomi compromised her family's influence. After her husband died, her sons were old enough to marry, and they chose Moabite women. As a Jewish mother, Naomi knew that inter-marriage was wrong. If Naomi protested, the Bible is silent; if she did anything to try to keep her sons from marrying outside the faith, again the Bible is silent. The only conclusion is that Naomi compromised her influence over her sons.

Naomi's Compromise

Wrong place	*went to Moab.*
Wrong priority	*money*
Wrong tolerance	*tolerated Moab culture*
Wrong counsel	*sent Ruth back to her old life and gods*

Naomi criticized God's provision for her. When Naomi came back to the Promised Land with Ruth, it was not a triumphant entry. Rather, Naomi came back with a critical spirit: "I went out full, and the LORD has brought me home again empty" (Ruth 1:21).

If Naomi died in Moab, her empty life would have had little notice. You would write *PRODIGAL* on her tombstone, and add a postscript that it was good she came home at last. But in the next few years, Naomi redeemed her lost years, and made a contribution for God that had eternal positive consequences. She guided her daughter-in-law Ruth to marry Boaz, and from that came the line of King David and Jesus the Messiah.

Naomi's Repentance Seen in Her Actions

Naomi recognized God's punishment. When Naomi went to Moab, she didn't see God's STOP sign. Rather, she walked out of the center of God's will into a heathen culture belittling God for eternal consequences. Her husband died. Even then it didn't seem that Naomi realized the unfolding plan of God in her life. Only when she made a decision to return to "The House of Bread" did she gain some spiritual insight into her past life. It's then she says, "The Lord has caused me to suffer and the Almighty has sent such tragedy" (Ruth 1:21, *NLB*).

Naomi guided Ruth toward her family heritage. When the women became desperate for food, Ruth assumed the position of a servant. She went out into the fields with other women to gather the sheaves that were missed by the harvesters. In Israel there was no such thing as welfare (see Deut. 24:19; Lev. 19:9), but the law provided that the poor could work in the fields behind the harvesters. They could keep what they picked up. Thus, Ruth was living on welfare.

God makes big things happen through little details. And as Ruth went out to look for a place to work, the Bible says she "happened" on Boaz's field. When the Bible says he was "A man of great wealth, of the family of Elimelech" (Ruth 2:1), it suggests that Boaz belonged to the same clan as Naomi's dead husband. They were related, but Ruth didn't know it.

Not only was Boaz a mighty landowner, but also he was a godly man. And when Boaz came into the field he greeted his workers, "The Lord be with you!" and they answered him, "The Lord bless you!" (Ruth 2:4).

There was a law in Israel called the Kinsman Redeemer. It was described as a levirate marriage, which required a man to marry the widow of his deceased brother to raise up the family name (see Deut. 25:5; Matt. 22:23-28). The fact that he was called a "Kinsman," the Hebrew word *goel*, indicates the man was able to buy Ruth and Naomi out of bankruptcy and/or bondage. He could pay off their debt and set them free; but at the same time marry his dead relative's widow, and re-establish the family line.

Interesting things happened in the barley field. Ruth worked hard but when Boaz arrived, she caught his eye. He asked the question, "Whose young woman is this?" Probably Boaz was in his forties while Ruth was in her late twenties.

The workers told Boaz how hard Ruth had worked all morning. It was then that Boaz invited her to eat lunch with his workers, taking some of their bread and dipping it in the sauce. She also is able to eat the cooked grain and drink from the water jug reserved for the workers.

Boaz wanted to keep her around so he said, "Do not go to glean in another field, nor go from here, but stay close by my young women" (Ruth 2:8). It's then that Boaz told his workers to drop extra sheaves for Ruth to glean. Boaz was smitten.

When Ruth got home that evening, she had much more grain than Naomi expected. As a matter of fact, Ruth had more grain than any of the other gleaners. Naomi was surprised and asked where she had been working. It's then that Ruth answered, "The man's name with whom I worked today is Boaz" (Ruth 2:19).

It's then that Naomi recognized the name Boaz. He was her relative, and now Naomi, who had no purpose, had a purpose. She who had no hope had a captivating hope. Naomi was going to make sure Boaz married Ruth.

Naomi directed Ruth towards family and spiritual redemption. The wise Naomi directed Ruth, telling her how to go to the threshing floor where Boaz would be separating the kernels of grain from their chaff. Boaz would work hard all day, but Ruth was to go there under the cover of darkness. While some people want to suggest Ruth was immoral in going to Boaz at night, nothing immoral happened. When Boaz laid down to sleep, Ruth came and slept at his feet, such as a servant would sleep. One of the main reasons was for protection and the other, to keep the master's feet warm. After all, a man sleeps better if his feet are warm.

In the middle of the night Boaz was awakened and realized a woman was lying at his feet. When he found out it was Ruth, she didn't wait for him to propose marriage, rather she asked him to perform his family duty to buy her and Naomi out of bankruptcy. She said, "Take your maidservant under your wing, for you are a close relative (i.e., *goel*)" (Ruth 3:9).

After agreeing to redeem Naomi and Ruth, Boaz sent Ruth home with a sack full of grain. What man doesn't like to buy things for his sweetheart?

Naomi counseled Ruth to have patience and trust. You can imagine the next morning how Ruth and Naomi sat around the house wondering what would happen. It was then that wise Naomi said, "Sit still, my daughter . . . for the man will not rest until he has concluded the matter this day" (Ruth 3:18).

The Blessing on Grandmother Naomi

Boaz went to sit in the gate, which is a phrase meaning he went to the place where business negotiations were made in the city. It was there that he negotiated to buy the property that had belonged to Elimelech and Naomi; i.e., buying it out of bankruptcy. And with the property came the obligation for Boaz to marry Ruth, and raise up the family line.

"Then the women said to Naomi, 'Blessed be the Lord, who has not left you this day without a close relative; and may his name be famous in Israel!

And may he be to you a restorer of life and a nourisher of your old age; for your daughter-in-law, who loves you, who is better to you than seven sons, has borne him'" (Ruth 4:14, 15).

After Boaz and Ruth were married, God gave them the birth of a son. The women of the community became so excited about this blessed event and they recognized the influence that Naomi had had to bring it about. The women praised the Lord, and insisted that the young baby Obed "would be famous in Israel." Obed means worshipper; the name is derived from a Hebrew word *ebed*, meaning a servant. The young child would be a servant of the Lord who worshipped the Lord.

1. Grandma Naomi is given more importance in the life of Obed than the mother Ruth. Notice how the women came to bless Naomi (see Ruth 4:14), and recognize the child is "kin" to Naomi. Naomi becomes the primary caregiver when the Bible says that "Naomi took the child and laid him on her bosom, and became a nurse to him" (Ruth 4:16). This does not refer to her actually feeding the child, which would have been impossible at Naomi's age. It probably means she was the primary caregiver for Obed, charged with feeding teaching life-skills to the young child.

Ruth would have been busy as the manager of a large household, which included servants in the home as well as in the field. Therefore, Ruth needed the help of Naomi in raising Obed.

But it also showed the closeness between a wife and her mother-in-law. Traditionally, there is some tension, both women vying for the close affection between the one man in their lives, i.e., the husband on the part of the wife and the son on the part of the mother. But here both women demonstrate love; just as they had previously shared Naomi's son, now they shared Ruth's son.

2. The child is identified with his grandmother, rather than his father or his mother. This is an unusual passage, for most sons are identified with their father. But there had been such a transformation in Naomi that she received the attention in the Bible text (see Ruth 4:14-17). Notice what they said: "There is a son born to Naomi" (Ruth 4:17). Even though Ruth was the birth mother, Naomi became the influential mother.

3. The child Obed would become famous in Israel. The word *famous* means, "name is proclaimed widely." And Obed became the great-grandfather of David. Perhaps the greatest name in

Old Testament history was David, so Obed became famous for his great-grandson.

4. The child gave Grandmother Naomi a purpose in life. When Naomi left for Moab, she became a compromiser. But when she returned to Bethlehem, she became a woman of conviction. What changed her? Sometimes hard times change a person. Other times, a *God encounter* changes a person. Still other times, people can change you. Perhaps it was the pure faith in Ruth that changed Naomi, because Ruth had a faith in God that Naomi lacked. This change in Naomi brought about her conviction.

Naomi came back to Bethlehem with no hope. She told Ruth, "Turn back, my daughters, go—for I am too old to have a husband. If I should say I have hope, if I should have a husband tonight and should also bear sons" (Ruth 1:12). You almost hear distress and resignation in her voice. But after Obed is born, she has new life. Notice what the Bible says: "May he [Obed] be to you a restorer of life" (Ruth 4:15).

When Naomi returned to the land, she had no spiritual energy; she had given up. She told her friends, "Call me Mara, for the Almighty has dealt very bitterly with me" (Ruth 1:20). But after Ruth bore a son, her life turned around. She was nourished. Again notice what the Bible says: "May he be to you a . . . nourisher of your old age" (Ruth 4:15).

Naomi's New Life

The respect of the town's women	*Ruth 4:14, 15*
The love of her daughter-in-law	*Ruth 4:15*
Restoration of hope and vision	*Ruth 4:15*
A grandson in the Messianic line	*Ruth 4:16*

5. Naomi gained the love of her daughter-in-law. Whereas there's usually some tension between mother-in-law and daughter-in-law, there is no tension here. "Blessed be the Lord. . . your daughter-in-law, who loves you, who is better to you than seven sons" (Ruth 4:14, 15). Every woman wants a son, because a son will please her husband. But here Naomi is blessed with a daughter-in-law who is better than a son; no, seven sons. Only God can give this type of love.

6. Grandma Naomi had the responsibility of influencing Obed. It appears that Naomi didn't do a good job raising her first son. She was a poor example taking him to Moab. She was a poor influence allowing her first son to marry outside the faith. But when given a second chance, she made sure that Obed was going to serve the Lord and worship Him. Even in the meaning of the name which young Obed assumed, this young boy would be faithful to God.

Lessons to Take Away

1. A grandmother has accumulated both natural and spiritual wisdom, love, and understanding. Because a grandmother has dealt with her children so many times, she has the wisdom and patience that's necessary with dealing with grandchildren. So, a grandmother can give better love . . . better counsel . . . and have more patience with her grandchildren. Whereas Naomi did not do a good job with her children the first time around, her accumulated wisdom and spirituality were present to influence her grandson, Obed.

2. Because grandparents have the advantage of seeing much of life, they should share as much as possible with their grandchildren. Most grandparents have seen the *mean* side of life, and they want to spare their grandchildren difficulties. Also, grandparents have had many heartaches, and they want to protect their grandchildren from as much sorrow as possible. On the other side, grandparents have had victories and they have shouted HALLELUJAH for answers to prayer. They should share all their experiences with their grandchildren. Can you see Obed's expression in Naomi's lap as she tells the young child about coming back to Bethlehem and having no food? Obed needed to hear how his mother worked hard in the fields to save life and limb. Also young Obed needed to know that his father provided a wonderful home for Ruth, his grand-mother and for him.

3. One of the greatest purposes when you reach retirement is to properly influence your grandchildren. What is retirement for ... shuffleboard ... fishing ... puttering around the house? While all these things are enjoyable, nothing is more eternal than invest-ing your time and wisdom in a grandchild. I (Elmer) have often said that a man in ministry should not retire, because ministry is your life. Ministry is what you would rather do than anything else. However, for working people in a job that is demanding and that "saps your life," you should look forward to retirement and the good things of life. However, the best thing for all people in retire-ment is to make your grandchildren the focus of your life, and to pour your influence into them.

4. Grandchildren give energy to grandparents. Naomi had many experiences to share with Grandson Obed. Before she left Bethlehem for Moab, she was an Ephrodite, meaning a blue blood in the com-munity. Because famine struck, she went to Moab where she was a foreigner and a minority. She had to go on welfare in Moab when her husband and two sons died. Naomi's next experience was as a returning prodigal where she and Ruth lived on Jewish welfare. Finally when Naomi became a grandmother, she was elevated in the eyes of the women in the community and given a place of re-sponsibility. It was here that the women said, "He shall be to you a restorer of life and a nourisher of your old age" (Ruth 4:15). Obed gave purpose to Naomi so that she had new energy in the sunset years of her life.

Today, your grandchildren can revitalize your life, because it will take all of your energy to entertain them while they visit your home. Your energy will be restored by their energy, because grand-children will run through your house, play in every corner, and will be constantly active until they leave. Then you fall exhausted into a chair to recuperate.

What is the *second* most delightful thing in the life of grandparents? It's when they see their grandchildren coming up the walk for a visit. Then you ask, what's the *first* most delightful thing in the life of grandparents? It's when you see the grandchildren leave, and you're exhausted.

5. A grandchild may give a second chance to a grandparent who messed up their child-rearing responsibilities the first time around.

Naomi didn't do the job right the first time. She and her husband focused on money during the famine, so they left the Promised Land and went to Moab. She didn't do a good job directing her sons because they married foreigners, marrying outside their Jewish faith. Some grandparents think they will suffer consequences the rest of their life because they messed up their child-rearing opportunity. Perhaps they may have a prodigal child, or they may have neglected a child, but when a grandchild comes along, grandparents have a second opportunity to "set the record straight." Naomi was given an opportunity to influence Obed. "Naomi took the child and laid it at her bosom, and became nurse to it" (Ruth 4:16).

Because Obed became the grandfather to David, we know that Obed must have been given good direction for his life; as was given to his son Jesse, and then to his grandson, King David.

6. Grandparents see life's big picture, seeing a long way into the past, and a long way into the future.

Naomi could look all the way back to Great-Grandmother Rahab, who chose to follow the God of Israel. That was a wonderful story of grace that she could tell to Obed. Then, Grandma Naomi could tell her *lifestory* to Obed, explaining about the consequences of disobedience. Her history became the basis for directing the future life of Obed.

Give the best of your life for the rest of your life.

When you get to be a grandparent, you usually have some accumulated money, and accumulated wisdom. You've been many places, done many things, and learned from them all. Walking through some grandparents' homes, you see trinkets, souvenirs, and mementos. Those things represent travel experiences, vacations, and the many jobs they've experienced. Don't forget scrapbooks. Grandparents have pictures of their children when they were babies, as well as pictures of their grandchildren. So realize that these pictures are more than just visual images; they represent the accumulated experiences of a life lived long, doing many different things and accomplishing many different goals. Now that you're a grandparent and have had these experiences, share your life, because your grandchildren need the best of you. What should you do? *Give the best of your life for the rest of your life.*

3

Asa:

Grandson of Maachah

Overcoming An Evil Grandmother

GRANDMOTHER—MAACHAH
FATHER—JEHORAM
SON—ASA

"Asa did what was right in the eyes of the LORD, as did his father David. And he banished the perverted persons from the land, and removed all the idols that his fathers had made. Also he removed Maachah his grandmother from being queen mother, because she had made an obscene image of Asherah. And Asa cut down her obscene image and burned it by the Brook Kidron."

1 KINGS 15:11-13

My name is Asa. I was born the year that my "great grandfather" King Solomon died. When I was a baby the palace was gloriously rich and all the guards had golden shields. All the utensils on the dining table were gold. I heard talk from the servants and my cousins about the "Golden Days" when Solomon was king. I knew one day I would be king, and I wanted everything to be as glorious as Solomon's reign when I became king.

But things did not go well when I was growing up. I remember that frightful time when Egyptian soldiers surrounded the walls of Jerusalem and threatened to kill us all. I was five years old and had terrible nightmares. My Grandpa Rehoboam gave the Egyptians all the gold to make their soldiers go away. He gave them the gold from the treasury, the gold cups off the table, and the gold shields of the soldiers. Everyone was very sad, but I kept thinking, "When I get to be king, it'll be glorious."

Things continued to get worse under Grandpa Rehoboam. There was no money, and he lost over half the kingdom—ten Northern Tribes—but he kept Solomon's Temple and Jerusalem. My Grandma Maachah was always complaining about having to go to the Temple to worship Jehovah. She fussed about the Ten Commandments, but I kept thinking, "I'll obey Jehovah when I get to be king." Grandpa Rehoboam worshipped foreign idols because he thought they'd protect him and make him rich. Grandmother Maachah loved the idols even more. I'll worship Jehovah when I become king.

When I was seventeen years old, Grandpa Rehoboam died and I thought things would get better when my father Abijah became king. But my father was a weak king. Grandma Maachah told my father Abijah what to do, just as she told Grandpa Rehoboam what to do, and they obeyed her. Grandmother Maachah said the people wanted to worship idols, so father built temples to Baal. But Grandma Maachah didn't just want idols; she wanted a woman-god. She built a great image to Asherah, the Canaanite mother goddess. She placed it in a grove of trees outside her apartment and burned incense there. I knew this was wrong. When I become king, I'll get rid of all the heathen idols.

My father Abijah didn't rule righteously; he let money go to his head, and he married many wives. He didn't please God. Within two years he died and I became king when I was only 21 years old. I knew that to have a glorious kingdom I'd have to get rid of idols and sin.

The first thing I did was to put Grandmother Maachah out of the palace and take away her crown. She would no longer be the queen mother. I broke her female idol into rubble and dumped it into a surrounding valley. I went into my father's house and destroyed all the idols that my father worshipped. Then I got rid of all of the Sodomites in the Baal temple and destroyed the temple itself.

I am going to be a godly king; I'll rule righteously for God. I want God's kingdom to be glorious again.

Maachah, an Ungodly Grandmother

Lesson to Take Away
Extreme abuses in grandparents can lead to the opposite
reaction in grandchildren, i.e., that godly grandchildren can come
from ungodly grandparents.

Let's look at Grandma Maachah; what kind of woman was she? When Grandpa Rehoboam married Grandma Maachah, he had no idea what kind of a wife she would be. Rebellious Maachah was the daughter of Absalom, the rebellious son of David who tried to steal the kingdom from David. Rebellious Absalom never lived by the rules; he made his own rules. Absalom never submitted to his father's rule; he wanted to rule over his father, David. He was a power-driven young man, and his daughter, Maachah, too was power-driven.

Absalom murdered his brother Amnon. It was not a murder of rage, but Absalom cruelly planned the murder and killed his brother. When his daughter Maachah married King Rehoboam, she too got rid of anyone in her way just like her father.

Absalom pretended to be loyal to his father, and smiled to his face, but behind his father's back, he was treacherous and turned people against David. When finally Absalom tried to kill David, one of David's generals had to kill Absalom.

So when Grandma Maachah married Rehoboam, what chance did Asa's grandfather have to become a godly man? None! Maachah was a vindictive, mean-spirited woman who would break every law—including God's law—to get her way. Maachah influenced her husband to evil, then she did the same thing to her son. "Now Rehoboam loved Maachah the daughter of Absalom more than all his wives and his concubines . . . and Rehoboam appointed Abijah the son of Maachah as chief, to be leader among his brothers; for he intended to make him king" (2 Chron. 11:21, 22).

Like father, like son. Now let's see what kind of man Grandpa Rehoboam was. Solomon was the wisest man on earth, and most people thought his son Rehoboam would be equally smart. But just as Solomon was betrayed by women, so too Solomon's son Rehoboam was betrayed by a woman, i.e., Maachah. Rehoboam was weak-willed, indecisive and couldn't be trusted to make the right decisions for God. Rehoboam wouldn't listen to the wise counsel of the elderly men who wanted young Rehoboam to reduce taxation on the people. The elders wanted Rehoboam to rule by love, not by force. But Rehoboam listened to his young hotheaded friends; he increased the taxes and the people rebelled. That's when Rehoboam lost the ten northern tribes into a separate nation.

Where was Maachah when this split occurred? Rather than counseling her husband to wisdom, the rebellious Maachah pushed her husband to rebel against the people he ruled.

Rehoboam's continuing sin corrupted the kingdom. Seldom do rebellious people learn wisdom and self-control, and Maachah continued to push her husband into a downward spiral of sin. "And he (\ [Rehoboam] did evil, because he did not prepare his heart to seek the Lord" (2 Chron. 12:14).

Grandma Maachah gave her son an evil name. The son that was to be the next king of Israel had two names. His first name was Abijah, which means, "The Lord is my Father." That might have been the name that Rehoboam called his son to satisfy the religious nature of the people. But Maachah gave him an evil name; she called him Abijam, which means, "My father is Yam." She named him for a Canaanite god of the sea.

Maachah supported sexual Sodom. When Abijam built a temple for Baal, the priest also instituted male prostitutes as a form of worship. This is one of the filthiest heathen practices ever. Someone has said that if sexual sins were a train leading to destruction, the caboose is homosexuality. When Asa became king, one of the first things he did was to get rid of the heathen temple, and the Sodomites. "And he banished the perverted persons from the land, and removed all the idols that his fathers had made" (1 Kings 15:12).

Maachah worshipped false gods. She not only provided a temple that the people asked for, and idols that they wanted, she also worshipped female Canaanite gods. This is terrible because Maachah had the royal blood of David flowing in her veins. But when Asa became king, he "removed all the idols that his father and mother had made" (1 Kings 15:12, author's translation).

Maachah secretly had a sexual goddess-idol. The Hebrew language suggests that the idol that Maachah had made was a female idol, i.e., a female sex god. "And Asa cut down her obscene image and burned it by the Brook Kidron" (1 Kings 15:13). Idols are not just mere small statues made of wood or stone. Rather, when people worship something made of stone, they worship the spirit or power the stone represents. Because Baal represented fertility, when farmers wanted their livestock to prosper, they worshipped the god of fertility hoping their flocks would produce offspring. What spirit of fertility was that? It was more than animism, i.e., a worship of neutral spirits; it was worship of demon spirits. An idol represents a spirit-demon, suggesting Maachah who kept her secret female idol outside her window was utterly evil and controlled by Satan.

Asa, a Godly Grandson

Extreme abuses lead to a radical reaction in some children. Grandpa Rehoboam sinned and started God's people down the path to evil. His son Abijah continued down that path. But a small boy growing up in the palace saw the abuses, and in his heart knew what was right. God was preparing Asa to be the first revival king of God's people. "Abijah walked in all the sins of his father, which he had done before him; his heart was not loyal to the LORD his God, as was the heart of his father David" (1 Kings 15:3). When young Asa saw all that his father did, he determined to be different.

I (Elmer) grew up in a home with an alcoholic father. While my father was good and kind, all of our family's money went for liquor. When I saw problems in our house, not enough money for rent, food, and basic necessities of life, I determined as a young boy I was not going to be like my father. I determined I would not be a drunk. I determined as a young boy sitting in a Sunday School class that I would never take my first drop of alcohol. In my case, abuses in my father led to reaction in this son.

God sovereignly prepared Asa for his godly rule. Even though circumstances formed Asa's attitude towards life, sovereignly the Holy Spirit was preparing a young boy to rule God's people. "Nevertheless for David's sake the LORD his God gave him a lamp in Jerusalem, by setting up his son [Asa] after him and by establishing Jerusalem" (1 Kings 15:4).

Asa began with reforms, and later introduced revival. Almost immediately upon his coronation, Asa began cleansing the temple. Aren't twenty-one-year-old young men reactionary? Don't they act first and think afterwards? Asa immediately began cleansing the nation. "He removed the altars of the foreign gods and the high places, and broke down the sacred pillars and cut down the wooden images" (2 Chron. 14:3). You can almost hear the whack of the axe, and the crunch of the sledgehammer. Asa probably didn't stay back in the palace and let his military leaders carry out the job. Young King Asa was probably standing on the steps of the temple of Baal directing his soldiers to destroy the evil place.

Asa demanded righteousness in the nation. Young men think they can demand allegiance from followers, but it's only the wise man who knows that people follow from their hearts, not from the law. "He [Asa] commanded Judah to seek the LORD God of their fathers, and to observe the law and the commandment" (2 Chron. 14:4). Even if commanding the people to follow the Lord doesn't always work, wouldn't you rather have Asa prodding the people to godliness, rather than his grandmother prodding them to lust after evil?

Asa raised and fortified the nation. Not only did Asa destroy the wicked infrastructures of the nation, but also the young king gave attention to military fortifications. "And he built fortified cities in Judah, for the land had rest; he had no war in those years, because the LORD had given him rest" (2 Chron. 14:6). It wasn't enough just to have stone walls for protection. "And Asa had an army of three hundred thousand from Judah . . . and from Benjamin two hundred and eighty thousand men" (2 Chron. 14:8). Asa raised a standing army of over a half million soldiers. With the forts and warriors, the nation had peace.

Asa's ultimate defense was in the Lord his God. When attacked, Asa didn't just depend upon his soldiers or high protective walls. When attacked, "Asa cried out to the Lord his God, and said, Lord, it is nothing for You to help, whether with many or with those who have no power; help us, O Lord our God, for we rest on You, and in Your name we go against this multitude. O Lord, You are our God; do not let man prevail against You!" (2 Chron. 14:11). Notice, he was not just defending his people and his nation; Asa was defending the Lord God. For he reminded God in his prayer that the enemy is attacking God Himself.

Asa led the nation in revival. Revival usually starts with a man or woman who is filled with the spirit of God, delivers the message of God. Azariah the prophet was that man that precipitated revival. "Now the Spirit of God came upon Azariah the son of Oded" (2 Chron. 15:1). This prophet Azariah went out to meet Asa to deliver unto him the message of God. "The Lord is with you while you are with Him. If you seek Him, He will be found by you; but if you forsake Him, He will forsake you" (2 Chron. 15:2).

Almost fifteen years after Asa the reforming king assumed the crown, he became the revival king. At age 36, Asa introduced the ministry of the Word of God. "For a long time Israel has been without the true God, without a teaching priest, and without law" (2 Chron. 15:3).

True, Asa had destroyed Baal's temple, but now he focused on the purpose of Solomon's Temple. What did Asa do? He "restored the altar of the LORD that was before the vestibule of the Lord" (2 Chron. 15:8). When the altar was restored, it was not just for show. The altar was the place where the blood sacrifice was offered for the sins of the people. Now Asa reminded people to come with their blood sacrifice for the forgiveness of sins. He now emphasized the spiritual nature of their religion, i.e., the relationship between a man and his God.

Asa celebrated the feast of the Lord. Asa exhorted the people to come up to Jerusalem and celebrate the feast by worshipping the Lord. Did they come? Yes, "when they saw that the LORD his God was with him "(2 Chron. 15:9). As a result, people obeyed the Lord and worshipped at the feast. "So they gathered together at Jerusalem in the third month, in the fifteenth year of the reign of Asa" (2 Chron. 15:10). And what did they do? "They offered to the Lord" (2 Chron. 15:11).

Asa led the people to renew their dedication to God. When the people came to Israel, it was not just enough to fill their heads with knowledge, or stir their hearts with devotion. He pledged their hand to obedience. "They entered into a covenant to seek the LORD God of their fathers with all their heart and with all their soul" (2 Chron. 15:12). So revival began when the people's hearts were right with God. "And all Judah rejoiced at the oath, for they had sworn with all their heart and sought Him with all their soul; and He was found by them, and the Lord gave them rest all around" (2 Chron. 15:15).

When the people entered into an oath with God, it was not because they were forced to obey God, as Asa had done when he first became king. This time the people willingly obeyed God and sought Him with their whole heart. "Then they took an oath before the LORD with a loud voice, with shouting and trumpets and rams' horns" (2 Chron. 15:14).

Lessons to Take Away

1. The Law has its exception. Some say, "Like father like son." But that's not always true. Some children grow up to be the opposite of their parents. Why do some children leave home walking in a different direction from their parents? Sometimes it's the influence of a godly man (King Josiah). Sometimes it's circumstances (Asa). Sometimes it's a death in the family (Mephibosheth). Sometimes the child identifies more with the loving nature of a mother than with the harsh nature of his father. Whatever the reason, there are always exceptions to the law "like produces like." Asa was not at all like his father and grandfather.

When Asa was a small child, "there was no peace to the one who went out . . . but great turmoil . . . nation was destroyed by nation, and city by city" (2 Chron. 15:5, 6). This means that the land was lawless, people were mugged in the streets, and women were not safe. When Asa was a small boy, he had personal guards because he was the son of the king. But the average person put their life into their own hands when they ventured out beyond their city. When

Asa was growing up, one city attacked another, and one nation attacked another. Young Asa saw lawlessness and danger everywhere, and wanted a different world. He remembered the stories he heard around the dinner table about the reign of his great-grandfather Solomon. Solomon did not have wars, but rather peace. That's what young Asa wanted. Peace!

2. Sometimes the evil influence of parents produces children more evil than themselves. This principle was seen in that Maachah was more evil than her father Absalom. While Absalom used guile and trickery in an attempt to gain the kingdom, Maachah used great force and ruthlessness. Both the father Absalom and the daughter Maachah were evil, but they expressed it in different ways. What can be seen from their lives? That while Absalom was evil, Maachah was twice as evil.

3. Sin is like a dead animal under the house; its stench can't be covered. Grandma Maachah was an evil woman who influenced her husband against worship of Jehovah God. She made him choose evil, and was the ultimate cause for the corruption of his kingdom. Her evil was expressed in the idol she kept in her yard, i.e., a female goddess. She might have reasoned that if male prostitutes were worshipping in the temple Baal, why could she not have a female idol to tickle her fancy.

But her idol was known by her grandson Asa. And one of the first things he did when becoming king was to get rid of her, her influence, and her female goddess.

How did Asa know about the female idol? Surely there must have been servants who talked about the female goddess, and word spread through the palace where a teenage boy named Asa listened to groups of servants talk. When people are addicted to gross sin, it's hard to cover it up, and it's hard to keep it quiet.

4. A family can be cursed to the third and fourth generation. God had promised that when the head of the family goes bad, the sin will continue to the third and fourth generation. "I the Lord your God, am a jealous God, visiting the iniquity of the fathers upon the children to the third and fourth generations of those who hate Me" (Exod. 20:5). In Asa's case, iniquity extended only to the third generation, not the fourth. Notice it went from Absalom à Maachah à Abijah à Asa. Young King Asa was the fourth generation from Absalom, and he turned out righteous.

5. God will sovereignly raise up righteous children. Out of a prostitute's sin have come some great godly preachers. Out of the homes of Atheists have come great Bible teachers. Out of dens where people fight God have come those who defend the name of God. "But where sin abounded, grace abounded much more" (Rom. 5:20). Technically the reference in Romans suggests that out of the disobedience of Adam and Eve came the gift of eternal life through Jesus Christ who died for the sins of the world (see Rom. 5:15-21). But this reference can also be applied to grandchildren. Where sin abounded in Rehoboam and Abijah, grace abounded much more in Asa.

6. Sometimes the grandchild has to deal with the sins of the grandparent. How hard was it for young twenty-one-year-old Asa to depose his grandmother? Did he have difficulty dealing with her sins? That's a question that can be difficult to answer. A child has natural love for his parents, so it's difficult to go against them. But at the same time, the child who loves God can obey God even more than parents. And a child's love of God can help him deal with the sins of his grandparents.

Jesus said, "If anyone comes to Me and does not hate his father and mother, wife and children, brothers and sisters, yes, and his own life also, he cannot be My disciple" (Luke 14:26). The word "hate" does not mean that you must turn your emotions against your parents when you follow Jesus Christ. That is not what Jesus meant. The word "hate" shows a comparison of two different worlds. You are to love God so much, and to follow Christ so devotedly, that in comparison your natural love for your parents will seem like hatred in light of your immense love for Jesus Christ.

7. A grandchild can become godlier as he/she grows older.
Asa began his rule as a young man who reformed the nation. He was carrying out the dreams he had as a young child growing up in the palace. But when he met the man of God, and was challenged with the Word of God, Asa responded to the next level in his spiritual growth. He took his reforms into revivals.

Asa began cleaning up his nation outwardly, but ended up dealing with the hearts of the people inwardly. He wanted them to follow God with all of their hearts, so he made them pledge a vow of commitment to seek God first and to follow Him with all their hearts.

4

Lois:
Grandmother of Timothy

Speaking the Words of Scripture into a Grandson

GRANDMOTHER—LOIS
MOTHER—EUNICE
GRANDSON—TIMOTHY

"Then he (Paul) came to Derbe and Lystra. And behold, a certain disciple was there, named Timothy, the son of a certain Jewish woman who believed, but his father was Greek. He was well spoken of by the brethren who were at Lystra and Iconium. Paul wanted to have him go on with him. And he took him and circumcised him because of the Jews who were in that region, for they all knew that his father was Greek."

ACTS 16:1-3

"When I call to remembrance the genuine faith that is in you, which dwelt first in your grandmother Lois and your mother Eunice, and I am persuaded is in you also."

2 TIMOTHY 1:5

"But you must continue in the things which you have learned and been assured of, knowing from whom you have learned them, and that from childhood you have known the Holy Scriptures, which are able to make you wise for salvation through faith which is in Christ Jesus."

2 TIMOTHY 3:14, 15

M y name is Lois, and I was born in Lystra, a small town in the mountains. It was an out-of-the-way place; not many people came to visit, so we didn't know a lot about what was happening in the world. There was not much culture or civilization in Lystra.

I was born of Jewish parents, but there were only a few Jewish families in Lystra. So, when it came to getting married, there were no Jewish boys available. A visiting rabbi said, "Better marry a Gentile man and drag him into Heaven than not marry at all." So I married a Gentile man. But my husband said that if we have a boy, he could not be circumcised or wear the Jewish Judenhut and the special kippah or prayer hat. But we had a beautiful black-headed girl and I gave her a Greek name, Eunice, meaning "commended well."

When it came time for Eunice to marry, she faced the same problems, the same limitations as I because there were no Jewish boys available, so she married a Greek. He told my daughter the same thing my husband told me, that if they were to have a son, he could not be circumcised or raised as a Jew, or be dressed as a Jew.

Both Eunice and I knew the baby would be a boy, and before he was born we dedicated him to God. We knew the stories of great Jewish heroes and we wanted him to be a great man of God. We knew the stories of Jewish boys who grew up outside the Holy Land—Moses . . . Daniel . . . Nehemiah . . . Ezra . . . and wanted our boy to be greatly used of God.

That little boy didn't stand a chance with both of us. When I was teaching, little Timothy learned the Law, the prophecies, and the great principles of God's Word. When Eunice was teaching him, he learned the psalms, to pray, and to passionately love God.

When he could barely run through the house, I taught him how to begin writing. I showed him how to cut the end off a feather for a pen. I showed him how to mix crushed charcoal and olive oil to make ink. We even made paper, crushing the papyrus reed into flat sheets. We dried the wet paper in the sun. Then I showed him to hold the feather between his forefinger and thumb and squeeze the barrel of the feather so the ink came out. He first wrote an *alaph*, the first letter of the alphabet. Then a *beth*, and next a *gimel*. For me, little Timothy copied the Law. For Eunice, little Timothy copied the Psalms and Proverbs.

One day Paul showed up in Lystra and gathered all the Jewish people together. There were not enough Jews in our town to have a synagogue, so we gathered in a large home. When Paul taught the Scriptures, I then believed that Jesus was the Messiah. I believed that Jesus was the Son of God. My daughter Eunice believed and so did Timothy. We believed because Paul showed us in the Scriptures that Messiah was to suffer, be killed, and rise again the third day.

Shortly after Paul arrived in town, outsiders showed up to argue with him. They attacked him and stoned him, dragging him outside town. Some of our people said he was badly hurt. Others said he was killed. I don't know what happened, but God did a miracle. Paul got up from the road, and walked back into town. We were all amazed . . . we rejoiced . . . we praised God.

That was two years ago, but now Paul is back in Lystra. He's heading off into the wilderness where it will be dangerous; he wants Timothy to go with him. That's not my decision, nor is it Eunice's decision. That's Timothy's decision. If Timothy goes along to help Paul, it'll be a dangerous trip. Timothy could even be stoned, like Paul was here in Lystra.

I hate to think about the death of a grandson, but I'm willing to give him up to the Lord Jesus Christ. Since Jesus suffered for us, what more could we do than give Him our all. And if Timothy gives his entire life to the Lord Jesus Christ, what better fulfillment can Eunice or I have than to realize that we taught a young man the Word of God, and now he'll use his life for the glory of God.

Grandmother Speaks into Young Life

Lesson to Take Away

When grandparents have limited resources and face barriers, they can motivate their grandchildren to greatness by speaking the Word of God into their lives.

Lois was influential in the life of her grandson, even though everything seemed to be against her. She had married outside the Hebrew religion, there was not a Hebrew synagogue to help teach her daughter and grandson, and she was isolated in a mountain town, cut off from civilization and cultural advantages.

Lois spoke the words of Scripture into Timothy so that he became an indispensable helper to the apostle Paul and the primary church leaders after the apostles had all died. The words Lois and Eunice spoke into Timothy became the foundation that guided Timothy's influential life.

If a grandmother speaks negative words, or words of discouragement into a grandchild, the young life will probably focus on what it *can't* do. If a grandmother speaks words of anger and bitterness into a child, the young person will probably be driven by temper or an irrational spirit. When a grandmother speaks words of greatness into a young child, that growing life will probably aspire to overcome difficulties.

Grandmother Lois married a Gentile. The Bible describes two women who were influential in the life of Timothy. The first woman was Lois who was married to a Gentile, just as her daughter Eunice also married a Greek. "A certain disciple was there, named Timothy, the son of a certain Jewish woman [Eunice] who believed, but his father was Greek" (Acts 16:1). This verse suggests the influence of a mother on a daughter. As the mother Lois had lived, so grew the daughter, Eunice. They both married Greeks. Maybe there were no eligible Jewish young men. Some think Lois might have rebelled against her Jewish upbringing to marry a Gentile in her desire to throw off her cultural shackles. If this is true, somewhere along the line Lois came back to her roots. Lois then taught her daughter Eunice Hebrew godliness, but also taught her grandson Timothy the Scriptures. However, this doesn't seem to be the case. Paul describes the "unfeigned faith" of Lois. She had a simple faith that was genuine and un-hypocritical. Lois probably married a Gentile because there were no other options.

Life in the mountain town of Lystra. When Paul went into a new town, he began preaching in the Jewish Synagogue, but no Synagogue is mentioned in Lystra. This is probably because there were not enough Jews to form a Synagogue (the Jewish rabbis insisted that it took twelve Jewish families to build a Synagogue).

Be a grandparent who overcomes insurmountable odds, and limited resources, and difficult circumstances, to influence your grandchildren to win battles, do exploits and achieve greatness for God.

Lystra was off the beaten path up in the mountains, and Roman historians indicate that there were very few Roman citizens that lived there. As a result, there were very little cultural advantages or Roman civilization. Also, Derbe and Lystra were not on the main highways, hence, travelers didn't pass through Lystra; only people who had business in Lystra visited there. As a result, the people of Lystra heard and experienced very little about the outside world.

Grandma Lois expected a son but got a daughter. Every Jewish woman expected her first child to be a son that she would dedicate as a rabbi. The next sons in the family would either be doctors, lawyers, teachers, or some other honorable profession. But Lois didn't have a son; she had a daughter Eunice, whose name means *commended*.

God commended the home of Lois and her husband with a little baby girl.

Like mother like daughter. Just as Lois had married a Gentile husband and probably agreed to raise her sons in Gentile tradition, her daughter Eunice had the same marriage bond and made the same type of agreement. When Timothy was born to Eunice, he was not circumcised. Later when Timothy began following Paul, the apostle "wanted to have him [Timothy] go on with him. And he took him and circumcised him because of the Jews who were in that region, for they all knew that his father was Greek" (Acts 16:3).

Grandma Lois had genuine faith. While some think she compromised in marrying a Gentile, that is probably not the case. Paul commends her, saying, "When I call to remembrance the unfeigned faith that is in thee, which dwelt first in thy grandmother Lois" (2 Tim. 1:5, *KJV*). The word *unfeigned* means genuine, and comes from the actors in a theater who played a role. When an actor would play a role on stage, he would wear a mask. But Lois had true faith, she was not playing a Christian role and she didn't wear a mask. Her faith was genuine.

Lois and Eunice poured their faith into Timothy. As they influenced Timothy, they taught the young child the Jewish Scriptures, making sure that he not only knew them in his head, but also accepted them in his heart. Paul told Timothy, "Continue in the things which you have learned and been assured of, knowing from whom you have learned them" (2 Tim. 3:14). The word "whom" is plural, suggesting Timothy was taught by both Lois and Eunice.

If one woman was strong in the devotional life, i.e., the Psalms, pouring spirituality into Timothy, the other woman was strong in the law or God's standards, pouring character into his life. Together the two women taught Timothy all of the Scriptures, and made him a strong disciple.

The word "knowing" is *oida*, which means Timothy didn't have just head knowledge, but innate knowledge. The women molded inner character into the life of young Timothy. He was obedient, not just when his mother was watching; he was obedient when no one was watching.

Character is always doing the right thing in the right way.

When Paul told Timothy to continue in the things that he had been assured, he was suggesting that the two women laid the foundation for Timothy's conversion. How Timothy began his Christian life is the way he continued serving the Lord.

Lois and Eunice began teaching young Timothy very early. Paul notes that, "from childhood you have known the Holy Scriptures, which are able to make you wise" (2 Tim. 3:15). The word "childhood" is *brethos*, which means embryo or a newborn baby. Long before Timothy could talk, the women began teaching him the Scriptures. Probably the women sang the psalms of Israel to him as they rocked or cuddled him in their arms. When they taught him to count the numbers, they probably repeated the Ten Commandments. When they taught him his ABCs, they probably identified with the great heroes of the Bible, i.e., A is for Abraham the father of faith, B is for Bathsheba the mother of Solomon, etc.

When Paul says that Timothy knew "the Holy Scriptures," he uses the Greek word *graphee*, which are the writings. This suggests first, a child would learn the Scriptures while copying the Scriptures. This is the way scribes learned the Bible. Timothy probably copied great portions of the Scriptures for his own personal possession. But second, the word *writings* is plural, suggesting that he didn't just learn the Scripture as an overall unit, but he learned each of the many parts of Scripture, giving attention to each book in the Old Testament. The women did their job well.

Lois and Eunice had a purpose in teaching young Timothy the Scriptures. They were to "make him wise unto salvation." Even a small preposition gives us insight into the way Timothy's grandmother and mother influenced him. The preposition "*eis*" suggests the women were always moving Timothy "into" salvation. They wanted him to be a good Jew in his heart, even though he didn't bear on his body the marks of circumcision.

Lois and Eunice prepared the spiritual foundation for Timothy's conversion. Eventually when Paul came to Lystra, Timothy believed in Jesus Christ. Why? Paul says, "When I call to remembrance the genuine faith that is in you, which dwelt first in your grandmother Lois and your mother Eunice, and I am persuaded is in you also" (2 Tim. 1:5). The pure, unfeigned faith of both Lois and Eunice was poured into the life of young Timothy, and he too had unfeigned faith. The soft feminine hands that caressed the baby's brow also pointed the direction in which the child eventually walked.

Paul Built on the Influence of Lois and Eunice

Some godly children are influenced by a godly father, and when that happens, God is glorified. In other occasions a godly child is influenced by a mother or a grandmother; and again, God is magnified.

Lois and Eunice believed that Jesus was the Messiah during Paul's first trip to Lystra. When Paul first came to Lystra (see Acts 14:6-23), he gathered the few Jews together and announced to them that Jesus Christ was the Messiah, that He died and rose again to give them new life. It was then that Lois and Eunice became believers, probably Timothy also. How do we know? When Paul arrived in Lystra on his second missionary journey, it was noted that Eunice was already a believer. "Then he [Paul] came to Derbe and Lystra. And behold, a certain disciple was there, named Timothy, the son of a certain Jewish woman who believed, but his father was Greek (Acts 16:1). The word *believed* is in the past tense, suggesting that Eunice believed in Jesus the first time Paul came to her city. Since the two women are joined in ministry in 2 Timothy 1:5, this suggests that Lois also believed on Jesus that first time Paul came to Lystra.

Timothy believed in Christ under Paul's ministry. Probably Timothy was saved under the Old Testament dispensation. He and the women were good believing Jews who followed the teachings of the Scripture. And in the Old Testament dispensation, if they had died before hearing about Jesus Christ, they would have gone to Heaven. How do we know this is true? Because when the message of Jesus was preached to them, they believed.

There's another reason to believe Timothy believed in Christ when Paul came to Lystra the first time. Twice, Paul calls him a son, i.e., spiritual son: "To Timothy, a true son in the faith" (1 Tim. 1:2) and "To Timothy, my beloved son" (2 Tim. 1:2). This is a relationship of love and esteem.

Timothy believed in spite of persecution. When Paul finally arrived at Lystra, he began preaching and not much happened. Then Paul healed a man at the city gate who was crippled from birth. This astounding miracle shocked the people of Lystra. They thought the gods had come down to them, i.e., Jupiter and Mercury. The people wanted to sacrifice an ox to Paul and Barnabas, but Paul rejected their offer and turned their attention to the God of Creation. He exhorted the people "that you should turn from these useless things to the living God, who made the heaven, the earth, the sea, and all things that are in them" (Acts 14:15). Young Timothy must have been impressed when he saw his substitute father-figure turn down crowd adoration and point people to the Living God.

But that's not the end of the story. Jews who hated Paul's message followed him from Antioch and Iconium and stirred up the town's people so that they stoned Paul. Notice who did the stoning. "The Jews . . . stoned Paul and dragged him out of the city, supposing him to be dead" (Acts 14:19). Timothy was probably an eyewitness to this execution.

Some believed that Paul was badly hurt but was able to get up and leave town the following day. They only "supposed" he was dead. Others believe Paul actually died. When he got up, it was God's raising him from the dead. This is probably the case, and later Paul suggests that during this occasion, he actually died and went to Heaven: "I know a man in Christ who fourteen years ago . . . such a one was caught up to the third heaven. And I know such a man—whether in the body or out of the body I do not know, God knows; how he was caught up into Paradise and heard inexpressible words, which it is not lawful for a man to utter" (2 Cor. 12:1-4). Because of what Paul saw and experienced in Heaven, he was given a "thorn in his flesh" for the rest of his life to remind him of his frailty and humanity.

Whether Paul was killed or not, Timothy witnessed the vicious persecution. But the attacks on Paul did not dampen Timothy's faith, nor did it turn away his decision to follow Jesus Christ. If anything, it probably put resolve in the young man's heart to be willing to suffer persecution also for God.

Later, Paul writes to remind Timothy of what happened in Lystra: "But you have carefully followed my doctrine, manner of life. . . persecutions, afflictions, which happened to me at Antioch, at Iconium, at Lystra" (2 Tim. 3:10-11).

Timothy was recommend by church leaders at Lystra. Not only was the young child Timothy well trained by Lois and Eunice, the people in the community respected young Timothy. When Paul came through the city on his second missionary journey, he invited Timothy to go with him to help him in ministry. The elders in the church at Lystra supported that decision. They not only thought it was a good idea, they were willing to go on record by ordaining young Timothy into ministry. Paul notes this event when he writes, "Do not neglect the gift that is in you, which was given to you by prophecy with the laying on of the hands of the eldership" (1 Tim. 4:14).

Timothy was ordained by Paul. After the leading elders in Lystra recommended Timothy for ministry, then Paul also laid hands on Timothy, setting him apart for ministry. Paul exhorted Timothy to keep on "stirring up the gift of God which is in you through the laying on of my hands" (2 Tim. 1:6). The words "stirring up" are in the continuous action, meaning Timothy was the type of a man who had to constantly challenge himself to use his spiritual gifts for the ministry of God.

Lessons to Take Away

When a grandmother has many limitations, she can still be a great influence for God through her children and grandchildren. In the natural realm there was not much that Lois and Eunice could do for the kingdom of God. But through young Timothy, their influence reached throughout the Mediterranean world. Their influence transcended time. When Paul needed help in his travels to the different churches, Lois and Eunice were there in the life of Timothy. When Paul was in prison in Rome, Lois and Eunice came to his assistance through Timothy. When Paul needed a preacher in the great city of Ephesus, Lois and Eunice answered the call through the ministry of Timothy.

Children do not become godly automatically; it takes initiative, focus, and commitment. Lois and Eunice made Timothy the focus of their life, so he received their love and attention.

John Wesley has given us good direction in how to teach young children. Stan Toler has shared with me the four principles John Wesley used to teach children.

Wesley's Principles of Teaching Children[1]

1. Early instruction.
2. Plain instruction.
3. Frequent instruction.
4. Patient instruction.

A grandmother's home can have great godly influence, even when a church is not available to help. Lois did not have the advantage of a full synagogue to assist in training Eunice or young Timothy. A synagogue is a place of teaching, where a rabbi would have taught the children the Hebrew language, the Law, as well as the basic necessities of life. Young Timothy probably did not have access to such a teacher or a rabbi. But what he didn't have in a male teacher, Lois and Eunice probably made up with "home schooling." As a matter of fact, they might be the prototypes of the modern home school movement. If so, perhaps young children will come from modern day home schools to equal the influence of Timothy.

Every grandmother needs the help of a godly male role model to influence her grandsons.

As great as the influences of Lois and Eunice were on young Timothy, Paul made all the difference in the world when he came on the scene. The apostle supplied the male role model. The preaching, ministry and example of Paul impacted young Timothy.

And why did Paul choose Lystra when there were so many cities in Asia Minor? He could have been led there by the sovereignty of God, but it might have been an answer to the prayers of Lois and Eunice who wanted young Timothy to be a great influence for God. And through the influence of Paul, Timothy became all that his grandmother and mother wanted him to become.

Giving great attention to small details in children's education will the influence their entire life. When Paul describes Timothy's knowing the "holy" writings, he implies that Timothy had copied the Scriptures, memorized the Scriptures, but more than that, believed the Scriptures and lived by the Scriptures. Grandma Lois and his mother Eunice had done their job well. When a grandmother can't be all she wants to be in life, at least she can be faithful in what God has given her to do. We don't know the dreams of Grandmother Lois, but we do know that she was faithful in training her young grandson, young Timothy. Because of her "unfeigned faith," she poured that faith into Timothy, and he was used in the foundation of missionary work throughout the Mediterranean world.

Note

1. Adapted from Stan Toler, *Lesson Five: Teaching to Influence Lives,* videotape Teacher Training Series.

5

Caleb:
Grandfather of an Unnamed Prodigal

How Prodigal Grandchildren Come from a Godly Grandfather

GRANDFATHER—CALEB
FATHER—OTHNIEL
GRANDSON—UNNAMED SON

"So the people served the LORD all the days of Joshua (and Caleb), and all the days of the elders (and Othniel) who outlived Joshua. . . another generation arose after them (unknown grandchildren) who did not know the LORD . . . Then the children of Israel did evil in the sight of the LORD, and served the Baals; and they forsook the LORD God of their fathers, who had brought them out of the land of Egypt; and they followed other gods from among the gods of the people who were all around them, and they bowed down to them; and they provoked the LORD to anger. They forsook the LORD and served Baal and the Ashtoreths" (Judg. 2:7-13, author's translation).

My name is Othniel. I am proud of my father-in-law Caleb, but my sons bring me grief; they don't follow the Lord. As a matter of fact, my sons have turned their backs on everything Caleb and I stand for. If you don't recognize my name Othniel, I am the first judge in a long line of famous people such as Gideon, Samson, and Samuel.

My father-in-law Caleb was born a slave in Egypt, and I remember him telling stories about a death angel going through Egypt killing all the first born. But the death angel passed over his house. Caleb told how he left Egypt and slavery triumphantly, how he walked through the Red Sea on dry land, how he followed the Shekinah-glory cloud through the wilderness, how he ate manna in the desert, and how God brought water from the rock. How could Caleb deny a God who did all that?

When our fathers conquered Cana, Caleb fought in all the battles. He was never wounded because God protected him. When he was eighty-five years old, he announced to Joshua that he wanted Mt. Hebron for his inheritance. God had promised Caleb the mountain. The enemy still occupied Hebron. Even at eighty-five years old Caleb wanted to go to conquer the mountain. My father-in-law was a great and mighty soldier for God.

What have I done? Nothing compared to my father-in-law. Caleb's generation conquered the Promised Land, but my generation didn't drive out the Canaanites. We didn't fully possess the land. If anything, we put the enemy in servitude and made them work our fields and become servants in our houses.

When my children came along, they didn't keep the Canaanites in servitude. Rather, my sons inter-married with their children, my sons allowed statues of Baal to be brought into their homes, and some of my sons tried to worship both Baal and Jehovah at the same time. My sons . . . Caleb's grandsons . . . began to act like the Canaanites, to eat the vile food the Canaanites ate, and to follow their practices. Many of our children stopped circumcising their young sons, and they didn't teach them the Ten Commandments, nor did they obey the Sabbath rest. They turned their backs on Jehovah.

My sons forgot that God delivered us from slavery in Egypt. My sons forgot that God led us through the Red Sea and into the Promised Land. My sons forgot that God give us this land.

They lost their pioneering spirit. They lost the convictions of their faith. And they lost their desire to be separate from sin.

My sons changed their worship of God to the worship of idols. They changed their opinion about themselves, and they changed their purpose in life from serving the Lord to becoming self-indulgent. Now they only live for themselves.

I am called the first judge because I went to battle against the king of Mesopotamia who put us into bondage. But now I am going to die. My children are not strong to fight, nor do they have the will to fight. Because they tolerated the Canaanites, now they are slaves to the Canaanites, and I am too old to help them. Who will deliver my children from bondage? Who will deliver them from their own weakness, and who can defeat the enemy? Unless God helps them, they cannot help themselves.

Why Do Grandchildren Go Bad?

Lesson to Take Away

Grandparents need to know why a grandchild becomes a prodigal. It happens when they forget where they come from, when they change what they have, and when they lose what is given to them.

Sometimes grandfathers are godly because they were delivered from a life of wretched sin. Perhaps a grandfather was a taxicab driver who knew how to get his customers to the wild parties for a price, and how to get patrons to find prostitutes, and how to make money off illegal activities. When the grandfather was born again, he repented of all of his sins, and went to an old-fashioned church altar where he prayed to receive Christ. Then he became a flaming witness for Jesus Christ, carrying a Bible in the front seat of his taxicab, standing in church to testify of salvation. He served Christ every way possible. That grandfather was delivered from slavery, just as Caleb was delivered from Egyptian slavery.

Then the cab driver had a child that he loved dearly. The child was raised in Sunday school, and she stood on the piano bench to sing solos in church. But the young child didn't have the same hatred for sin as her father, the "born-again cab driver." When she asked, "What's wrong with going to a rock concert?" The father refused to let her go because he knew there would be drugs, sex, and violence. The second-generation young Christian girl didn't hate sin as her father; she served Christ to please her father.

Then a grandchild was born to the cab driver. The grandchild didn't know about the grandfather's life in sin and didn't know about his radical conversion. Therefore, the grandchild didn't separate himself from sin, but rather ridiculed his grandfather. He lived more like the unsaved at high school than like the young people at church. Finally, the grandson ended up in the sins that his grandfather once committed.

When a grandchild goes bad, who's fault is it? Maybe it's not what parents and grandparents did wrong, but what they didn't do right.

An early church father said, "Each generation must stand on the shoulders of those who have gone before—and reach higher." If grandchildren do not reach spiritually higher than their parents, are they destined to fall lower?

Caleb was forty years old when he was sent out as a spy, and at age eighty-five the land of Israel was divided among the twelve tribes of Israel. Caleb boldly asked for the mountain known as Hebron and the hill country where the feared Anakin lived. Even at age eighty-five Caleb felt that he could fight and win a battle against his enemies.

Caleb gave his daughter, Aachsah, to Othniel in marriage. After Caleb died, Othniel became the next ruler of Israel. Othniel was great but not as great as his father-in-law, Caleb. Neither were as great as Moses. Because of diluted leadership, the people began to drift spiritually. When the people wandered from God, King Cushan-Rishathaim of Mesopotamia invaded Israel and put the nation into bondage.

"Therefore the anger of the LORD was hot against Israel, and He sold them into the hand of Cushan-Rishathaim king of Mesopotamia; and the children of Israel served Cushan-Rishathaim eight years. When the children of Israel cried out to the LORD, the LORD raised up a deliverer . . . Othniel . . . and the Spirit of the LORD came upon him, and he judged Israel. He went out to war, and the LORD delivered Cushan-Rishathaim king of Mesopotamia into his hand" (Judg. 3:8-10).

Othniel drove out the enemy and reestablished the government. He became the first of the political-religious rulers known as *judges*. Because of Othniel's victory, Israel had a generation of peace, i.e., forty years (see Judg. 3:9-11).

An Unknown Grandson

Othniel probably had children, but we do not know their names. If Caleb had a grandson, we do not know his name. But we do know that the generation of grandson sinned against God.

Why is it that godly grandparents sometimes have prodigal grandchildren? Sometimes a man of God will serve the Lord faithfully, yet his grandson will drift from the Lord. What happens in the Christian life also happens in the natural world.

"And the people served the Lord all the days of Joshua (and Caleb) and all the days of the elders (and Othniel) and outlived Joshua . . . There arose another generation after them that know not the Lord . . . they did evil in the sight of the Lord, and served Baalam . . . and the anger of the Lord was against them, and delivered them into the hands of the nations around about them" (Judg. 2:7-13, author's translation).

From rags to riches to rags in three generations. In the business world, a grandfather may begin financially poor, but with tremendous drive and self-discipline, he works hard to accumulate a fortune. Then his son enjoys the fortune, but never experiences the financial depravity that his father suffered, so he doesn't have to work hard. The son doesn't appreciate his inherited wealth. The son may admire the inheritance of his father, but he doesn't learn the value of work that is necessary to make money, so his son—the third generation—can't keep the inheritance that his grandfather made. The grandson squanders the family fortune and returns to the poverty of his grandfather.

From sin to salvation to sin in three generations. Sometimes a wicked grandfather is caught in the clutches of sin, but through a miraculous conversion, is transformed. He turns from sin and aggressively serves the Lord. Then he has a son who enjoys his Christianity, but doesn't have the deep convictions of his father. He lives on his father's faith. Finally a third generation grandson is enticed by sin, ventures into iniquity, and ends up addicted to the same sin from which his grandfather was delivered.

Children born into families of first generation Christian pioneers begin to change their church before they reach adulthood. First generation soul winners become educators to make the next generation conform to their ideals. But the second generation holds its convictions less fervently than their pioneering parents, whose convictions were formed in white-hot Christian battle.
The third generation has even more difficulty separating itself from the world.
—Adapted from Sociologist Richard Niebuhr

From slavery to serve the Lord to slavery in three generations. Grandfather Caleb was a slave in Egypt, but demonstrated great character in serving the Lord. His son-in-law Othniel was also a leader in Israel, but the people under Othniel compromised their faith and drifted back into sin. God used Othniel to deliver his generation. But the third generation of unknown grandsons was enticed by sin, and became a slave to the nations around them.

Why is it that grandchildren will leave the faith of their fathers? Why is that grandchildren will turn their backs on the good things they see in the Christian testimony of their grandparents? Perhaps the problem is threefold.

1. Christian grandchildren forget where they came from.
2. Christian grandchildren change what they have.
3. Christian grandchildren lose what is given to them.

What the Prodigal Grandson Forgot

The prodigal grandson forgot they had been slaves and that God delivered from Egypt. Why is it that God's children forget that they had been slaves to sin? Perhaps because Christians begin thinking they are good in their own strength, so sin slips up on them and puts them into bondage. They forget that they belong to God, so they start playing with sin. When Christians forget the terrible results of sin, they are attracted by its allurement and give in to their lust.

The prodigal grandson forgot God guided them through the Red Sea and the wilderness. Once God's people settled down in the land, they became self-sufficient. They forgot that they would have been lost in the wilderness if it were not for God. They forgot that God led them day-by-day through the wilderness by the Shekinah glory cloud. In the wilderness God fought the battle for them against Amalek, God fed them manna each day, God gave them water out of the rock, God healed their diseases, and God ultimately brought them into the Promised Land.

Why is it that our Christian grandchildren become prodigals? Can they forget that God's Spirit led their parents to a better life, that God provided for their daily bread, that God answered their prayers, that God protected them from the Evil One, and that God satisfied them with His presence? To backslide, a prodigal grandson has to climb over the memories of his parents and grandparents. The prodigal grandson has to stumble over the work of God to fall into sin.

The prodigal grandson forgot God gave them the Promised Land. God put Israel in the land and told them to be separate from the nations round about them. God wanted to be glorified through the worship of Israel. But once in the land, the prodigal grandchildren began flirting with the heathen nations, they began worshipping heathen gods, and they began adapting to heathen ways.

In the same way, Christian grandparents forget what the God of their grandfathers had given to their parents. They entertain themselves by the world's stage, listen to the world's music, eat from the world's delicacies, and think the world's thoughts. When they are completely influenced by the world, is it no wonder that they go live in the world?

What the Prodigal Grandsons Changed?

The prodigal grandsons changed their worship of God into idol worship. They probably didn't begin worshipping idols immediately; compromise usually involves a long, slow process. First they may have become disenchanted with the provision of God, and then they didn't properly handle problems and reverses that naturally happen in life. Then their prayers weren't answered the way they expected, and they saw the heathen seeming to get more results by worshipping Baal than they were getting. Probably the prodigal began by adding an idol shelf in his home, keeping it separate from the Torah (Law). But slowly the two got put together, until the prodigal grandson couldn't tell the difference in his mind between praying to Baal or Jehovah. So finally, he substituted an idol for the Lord.

The same thing happens to Christian grandsons. They probably never mean to deny the Lord or to forsake Him, but slowly the same process happens to them that happened the Othniel's unnamed grandchildren. They become disenchanted with church, and disappointed in its leaders. Their prayers were not answered as they expected, and church became a meaningless experience. They found themselves enjoying the world's music, more than hymns. They found themselves enjoying the world's entertainment, more than fellowship with Christians. Is it no wonder that they finally stopped being a hypocrite and threw off Christianity for the ways of the world?

The unnamed prodigals changed their opinion about themselves. After living in the Promised Land for quite a while, they no longer thought of it as "God's land," but it became "their land." They slowly began taking credit for "their crops," and "their children." Finally, it was "their wealth." They no longer saw themselves as delivered slaves from Egypt. They became satisfied plantation owners sitting on the veranda. When they no longer needed God, they threw Him over for a different lifestyle, a different worship pattern, and a different value system.

The unnamed prodigals changed their relationship to sin. Grandpa Caleb was completely separated from sin, and when the ten spies came back from the Promised Land to mislead the multitude, Caleb stood for God. He "rent his clothes" (Num. 14:6) and cried out, "Only do not rebel against the LORD" (Num. 14:9). Grandpa Caleb would have nothing to do with compromise. But Caleb's unnamed grandsons didn't separate themselves from the world, but brought the Canaanite into their homes as house servants, then later inter-married with them; finally Caleb's grandchildren became like the Canaanites. What the third generation sons didn't realize was that a person can never become an equal partner in a marriage with sin; but rather they become a servant of sin. The book of Judges describes them being in "bondage" under the hand of the "oppressors."

What the Prodigal Grandsons Lost

The prodigal grandsons lost their pioneering spirit. The first chapter of Judges describes how Israel possesses the land after conquering it. Each of the tribes went out to possess the land given to them. But constantly the phrase is repeated in that chapter, "They did not drive them out" (Judg. 1:32). This means they did not defeat and eliminate the Canaanites. They lost their will to fight; they lost their passion to possess the land; they lost their pioneering spirit. They settled in the Promised Land, but didn't completely obey the Lord to get rid of the heathen.

The prodigal grandsons lost their conviction and belief. Israel fought thirty-one battles in the book of Joshua, and won thirty-one times (initially they lost the battle of Ai, but came back to capture the city). Their strength was not their warlike spirit, neither was Israel trained as soldiers. As a matter of fact God said, "Now these are the nations which the LORD left, that He might test Israel . . . all who had not known any of the wars" (Judg. 3:1). God wanted these grandchildren who didn't know how to fight to learn the experience of victory. Israel's strength was not its armaments or battle skill, but it was its knowledge and dependency upon God. God gave them victory but "They forsook the Lord and served Baal" (Judg. 2:13).

Spiritual grandfathers know their strength comes from God, i.e., strength to overcome sin, strength to obey God's law, and strength to do God's will. However, when they lose their trust in God, they have no strength to stand against the world. So what do prodigals do? They go into the world.

The prodigal grandsons lost their desire for separation from sin. God had wanted His people to be holy, which means to "cut off" or to "separate." God made covenants with His people; the word *covenant* means to "cut off." God wanted to "cut" Israel off from reliance on the heathen, or even becoming like the heathen. God's desire was that Israel would be "holy unto the Lord." But the unnamed grandchildren lost their passion for holiness. "They turned quickly from the way in which their fathers walked" (Judg. 2:17).

Usually the first place where prodigal grandchildren slip is in their attitude towards sin. They begin asking what's wrong with drinking alcohol, or smoking, or other negatives from which Christians have separated themselves. They begin finding satisfaction in the attractions of the world, their entertainment, food, and recreational drugs or other habit-inducing diversions. After a spiritual grandson loses his passion for separation from sin, it is an easy slide into the lifestyle of the world.

When Your Grandchildren Are Prodigals

The word prodigal comes from an original French word *prod-forth*, which can mean (1) to drive away, or (2) to squander, be extravagant, or be characterized by wasteful expenditure. When a grandchild spends lavishly or foolishly, they can be called a spend thrift. They "spend" the life on iniquity. However, the term *prodigal* in Scriptures suggests a child who doesn't appreciate the lifestyle of his home, nor the necessities that have been provided by his home. A prodigal child has an attitude problem. First, they have rejected what has been provided for them in their home, and second, they think that life away from the home will be immensely better. Therefore, a prodigal runs away to waste his or her resources on a lifestyle that appears to be superior. Sometimes prodigals waste their inheritance (i.e., money given by parents). Other times a prodigal wastes their physical resources (i.e., give their life to drugs, alcohol, or sexual pleasures), or a prodigal can waste advantages (won't go to college, or enter the advantages of their parents). When a child or grandchild becomes a prodigal, what can a grandparent do?

Become an intercessor. When you see a grandchild beginning to wander or heading toward a prodigal's life, you must become their intercessor, crying out to God for their future. When no one else will pray for the child, you must do it. Remember, Isaiah "saw that there was no man, and wondered that there was no intercessor" (Isa. 59:16).

When no one was concerned about Sodom and Gomorrah, Abraham interceded in the presence of God. When the nation of Israel was going to be blotted out, Moses the intercessor refused, saying, "Blot me out of Thy book first." When the entire world needed saving, Jesus became the intercessor on the night before His death: "I pray for them. I do not pray for the world but for those whom You have given Me, for they are Yours" (John 17:9).

Jesus has promised that if *two will agree*, you will get what you ask. So, the two of you (grandparents) enter into an intercession-covenant for your prodigal grandchild. "Again I say to you that if two of you agree on earth concerning anything that they ask, it will be done for them by My Father in heaven" (Matt. 18:19).

Direct their eyes away from immediate gratification. One of the reasons children become prodigals is because of what they see. They see the enticement of sin, they see the pleasures of money, they see the grass is greener on the other side of the fence. Along with what they see in the world, they see "legalistic rules" at home. They feel they can't have what they want and they feel rejected by their parents. They feel their parents are denying them the best things in life, so they become prodigals.

But as a grandparent, you have a different relationship to grandchildren. You don't have to enforce the household rules, so the prodigal children won't reject you along with rejecting their parents' rules. Therefore, the prodigal grandchild may be open to you; you may have an opportunity to help them see life differently. Help them form dreams that are not tied to the lust of the eyes, the lust of the flesh, and the pride of life (see 1 John 2:15, 16).

Share stories of their parents' struggles. Since you raised the parents of prodigal children, let grandchildren know about the struggles their parents had in life. Since sin is a cruel taskmaster, remind them of the consequences that their parents had to pay; also remind them of the rewards for right conduct.

Create biblical heroes in their heart. Remind your grandchildren of heroes from the Bible, and how they overcame difficulties to be used greatly of God. David was chased in the wilderness thirteen years before he became king. Jacob spent twenty years waiting outside the Promised Land because of his lies and the death threat of his brother. Paul had to spend three years in Damascus and the wilderness before he could go to Jerusalem. Even when Paul got to Jerusalem, his past became a death threat and he had to leave the holy city. Give your grandchildren modern-day Christian heroes. Speak well of Christian leaders, describe their accomplishments, and pray for Christian leaders in the presence of your grandchildren.

Help prodigal grandchildren accept their limitations and difficulties. Obviously a prodigal grandson wants to run away from trouble. Remind them everyone has trouble. "Man who is born of woman is of few days and full of trouble" (Job 14:1). Prodigal grandchildren need to accept the fact that life is a journey through troubles—life is not a weekend vacation, nor is life a day off from school.

Remind them of God's past work. A prodigal grandson needs to know your *life story*, how God has worked for you in the past, and how God has delivered you from difficulties. They need to hear how God has worked in the life of your children, i.e., the parents of prodigals. Help them to see that God works through the difficulties of life. Your grandchildren may be like Joseph, who was mistreated by his brothers, sold into slavery, and ended up in prison. Show your grandchildren how God can work in their life as He worked in the life of Joseph. The hand of God was on Joseph's life; "But as for you, you meant evil against me; but God meant it for good, in order to bring it about as it is this day, to save many people alive" (Gen. 50:20). Your prodigal must know God has a plan for his/her life!

6

Joash:

Grandson of Athaliah

Hallelujah for Godly Aunts and Uncles

GRANDMOTHER—ATHALIAH
FATHER—AHAZIAH
GRANDSON—JOASH

"Now when Athaliah the mother of Ahaziah saw that her son was dead, she arose and destroyed all the royal heirs of the house of Judah. But Jehoshabeath, the daughter of the king, took Joash the son of Ahaziah, and stole him away from among the king's sons who were being murdered, and put him and his nurse in a bedroom. So Jehoshabeath, the daughter of King Jehoram, the wife of Jehoiada the priest (for she was the sister of Ahaziah), hid him from Athaliah so that she did not kill him. And he was hidden with them in the house of God for six years, while Athaliah reigned over the land."

2 CHRONICLES 22:10-12

I am a seven year-old boy and I have healthy milky-clean colored skin, because I stay in doors all the time. I live in an apartment in the Temple area, where the priests live. Every night my Uncle Jehoiada and Aunt Jehosheba take their bedrolls out of the closet and spread them on the floor to sleep. I sleep in the closet. Uncle Jehoiada said hiding in the closet will save my life.

I can't go out of our room, and I couldn't even look out the window until Aunt Jehosheba put a plant there, so I could peek between its branches. That way no one can see me.

My aunt and uncle told me how my evil grandmother Athaliah killed all my brothers and sisters. My grandma worships Baal; she hates God and the Ten Commandments. She will not bring a blood sacrifice to God for her sins, and does not observe the feast days.

Uncle Jehoiada can't sacrifice for the sins of the people anymore, because Grandma Athaliah won't let anyone bring sheep into the Temple. When the people bring a trespass coin to the Temple, the guards seize it and take it to my grandmother. I don't know why she doesn't follow God.

Auntie and Uncle tell me that I've got royal blood flowing in my veins, that I'm the only seed left of the tribe of David. They tell me that one day I'll sit on the throne. They call it David's throne. I spend a lot of my time learning to read and write. Moses said that every king should make his own copy of the Torah and keep it by his side to rule Israel. So, Aunt Jehosheba has already taught me how to write, and I've begun copying my own scroll of the Torah. One day Auntie took some charcoal from the fire, mixed it with olive oil and made this black icky liquid. Then she showed me how to cut off the end of a feather. When I squeezed the barrel of the feather and stuck it in the black ink, it sucked that ink right up into the barrel. Then I learned how to slowly squeeze the barrel again, making letters on some soft leather skin.

My favorite Scripture was written by my grandfather, nine times ago. Uncle Jehoiada says that I am nine generations from

David who wrote, *"The Lord is my Shepherd, I shall not want, He maketh me to lie down in green pastures. He leadeth me beside still waters; He restoreth my soul."*

I believe in the Lord, just like my nine times Grandfather David, and I want the Lord to lead me, just like He led David when he was a shepherd boy.

One day Uncle Jehoiada came rushing in; I could see his face was serious. I knew something important had happened. Aunt Jehoidabeath bought a beautiful white linen tunic for me, one that I had never worn before. "I made it especially for this day," she said.

"What day is this?" I asked, but she just smiled.

They walked me briskly down the hallway; I had never been that far from my room. I saw soldiers everywhere. They had tall heavy spears, large shields and helmets on their head. I wanted to stop and look at the soldiers, but Uncle Jehoiada said we had to hurry.

I was brought into the large court; the walls were golden and shiny, not plain white like the apartment where I had lived. Everyone was rushing about. There were two soldiers standing guard at each door, which we passed. I liked the guards because they looked at me and smiled. I smiled back.

"Stand him by the pillar," Uncle Jehoiada told me. I heard him say that the king is always crowned standing next to the pillar. *"Was that me?"* I thought.

They brought a long, royal red robe and attached it about my neck, but it was way too big for me. I looked behind me and it stretched all the way around the gold-covered pillar.

Then I saw them. There must have been a hundred soldiers standing shoulder-to-shoulder all around the room. They formed a wall so tight that no one could get through them. Uncle Jehoiada said to them, "If anyone tries to get through the ranks, kill them."

"Wow, this is serious." I didn't know what was happening, but this was not just your average day.

Then Uncle Jehoiada brought a crown, a beautiful gold crown with sparkling jewels. It was the most beautiful thing I had ever seen. When Uncle Jehoiada put it on my head, it was too big. The crown slid down around my ears and covered my eyes. Some of the priests smiled, but I knew they were not laughing at me. I knew this was the crown that was worn by men who ruled the nation for God.

Then everyone started shouting: *"GOD SAVE THE KING! . . . GOD SAVE THE KING! . . . GOD SAVE THE KING!"* I had never heard so much noise in my life. They continued shouting, *"GOD SAVE THE KING!"*

I looked around to find the king, then I realized everyone was looking at me. I was the king! Later, Uncle Jehoiada told me what a special time this was, but I didn't realize it then.

They handed me this long golden pole, but I didn't know what it was. They told me that it was a scepter, but I had never seen a king or queen rule, so I didn't know what to do with the scepter. I grabbed it with both hands, but Uncle Jehoiada told me to hold it toward the people with one hand, saying, "That's the way kings rule."

Next Uncle Jehoiada had a large scroll; I recognized what it was. It was the Torah because I had been copying my Scripture from a scroll just like it. Uncle Jehoiada said, "You'll keep this Law by your right hand to guide you in ruling Israel." I nodded my head, knowing what that meant.

The people began clapping again, even louder they shouted, *"GOD SAVE THE KING!"* Trumpets began to blow, louder than ever before, and more trumpets than ever before. For a long time the people shouted . . . clapped . . . and the trumpets were blowing.

Then suddenly, everything got quiet. The people looked toward a small door that led to the king's palace. There was Grandma Athaliah; she had come in with several of her soldiers. I saw her before she saw me. Grandma Athaliah was really mad, I could see it in the way she walked. She was stomping mad. When she saw me, she yelled, "TREASON . . . TREASON . . . TREASON." Grandma Athaliah began to tear her clothes.

Our soldiers ran and formed a line, a tight line between her and me. They were shoulder-to-shoulder, and so big that I couldn't see what happened.

Uncle Jehoiada yelled out over the noise, "Take her outside the Temple; don't kill her in the House of God." I couldn't believe my ears; they were going to kill my grandmother.

The soldiers from Uncle Jehoiada rushed over and surrounded Grandma and her guards. I heard their swords drop to the ground. Men were yelling; I saw them head towards the door that leads to the stables. That's where the horses are kept. Later, Uncle Jehoiada told me that they killed Grandma Athaliah there in the stables.

"Why?" I simply asked.

"Because she killed all your brothers and sisters and cousins." Uncle Jehoiada went on to explain that she killed over 70 people in my family, everyone who was in the seed of David. "She killed them all, except me." Then Uncle Jehoiada said, "If we didn't kill her, she would gain sympathy from some followers who would try to kill you."

That was a frightful day for me. First, it was scary because I didn't understand what it meant to be king of God's people. But it was also scary because Grandma Athaliah would have killed me if she could.

I'm not going to be like Grandma Athaliah. I will rule God's people the way God wants me too. I will open the Temple and allow people to come and to make sacrifice for their sin. I will repair the house of God and make the sanctuary the most beautiful place in Israel.

Grandma Athaliah worshipped at the Temple of Baal, but I know that honoring Baal is wrong. I will tear down the Temple of Baal and get rid of all the priests of Baal. The only place of worship in my kingdom will be the Lord's Temple; that's the place where I spent the first seven years of my life. And like David my grandfather nine times said, "I want to live in the house of the Lord forever."

A Good Grandson Comes from an Evil Grandmother

Most of us have a comfortable image of a grandmother, i.e., plump woman . . . a dash of flour on her nose . . . making cookies . . . or sitting peaceably by the fire, knitting a sweater. The word *grandmother* means . . . pleasure . . . contentment . . . coziness . . . satisfaction . . . and solace. But that was not the experience of young Joash. He had an evil grandmother who was mired in filthy worship of an obscene god, who was vindictive of anyone who was righteous, and punished all who were godly.

Joash faced the challenge of understood generational sins. God had said that He would "visit the iniquities of the fathers [and the mothers] upon the children under the third and fourth generation under them that hate Me" (Exod. 20:5). Young Joash's great grandmother was Jezebel, the personification of wickedness. When anyone describes a vile woman, they use the adjective, "She was a Jezebel."

The daughter of Jezebel was Athaliah, and the daughter was more wicked than Jezebel if it's possible to be more wicked than the wickedest woman ever. Athaliah married Ahaziah, a wicked king. So, here was young Joash, the first child born after three generations of evil; what would become of him?

The great-grandmother Jezebel was a corruptor. King Ahab was an evil but weak-willed man, and at times lacked conviction. He married Jezebel, a woman from Phoenicia (a land we know today as Lebanon). What do we know about Jezebel? When she married into God's people, she immediately built a sanctuary to Baal, the heathen god that she worshipped (see 1 Kings 18:19). Next, Jezebel hired priests and prophets to worship and serve in the temple of Baal. They were identified as *her* prophets and priests (see 1 Kings 18:22).

The godly prophets who served Jehovah stood against Jezebel, denouncing and prophesying against her. What did she do? She killed those godly men who opposed her (see 1 Kings 18:4).

When Elijah had his great confrontations on the top of Mount Carmel, Jezebel's priests could not pray and bring fire out of Heaven. But God's man—Elijah—was able to pray down fire out of Heaven that consumed the sacrifice, and the altar. It had not rained for three and a half years—a judgment of God—but when Elijah began to pray, a great storm deluged the nation. Ahab jumped into his chariot and headed home to tell his wife Jezebel what happened. When Jezebel heard what happened, she threatened to kill Elijah (see 1 Kings 19:3).

Grandmother Athaliah was a usurper. How is it that some children become evil like their parents, while other children react to the excesses of sin and become godly? No one can completely answer that question. However, you get a clue by looking at a child's self-perception. When the child's ego identifies with an evil parent, the child will probably commit every sin that the parent did, and more. Just as godliness wants to stand on the shoulder of a righteous person to reach higher, so too wickedness wants to walk in the shoes of an evil person and trod lower.

Grandmother Athaliah was from the Northern tribes of Israel, a nation that had nothing to do with the southern nation of Judah. The Temple was located in the Southern Kingdom; that's where the priests sacrificed to God, and the people came to worship in the presence of God. Also, God promised that the Messiah would come through Judah, the Southern Kingdom.

Since the Southern Kingdom was more godly than the Northern Kingdom, it should have been a wall of separation between the two, and those in the Southern Kingdom should have separated themselves as far away as possible from the influence of the North. But the Southern King Jehoram married Athaliah from the North. Not only did King Jehoram compromise his walk with God, he went to bed with an evil woman, and became despicable under the influence of his wife Athaliah.

When Jehoram died, Athaliah influenced the kingdom through her son Ahaziah. When Ahaziah unexpectedly died, Athaliah looked around for the next king to influence. Her weak husband whom she controlled was dead. Her weak son that she controlled was dead. She couldn't find a son or grandson to take the throne. Since she had no pawn to control and she didn't have time to mold another son into her image, she decided to become the next ruler. So, she usurped the throne for herself. Why was this wrong? Because Athaliah was not in the Messianic line of Messiah, i.e., a line of David. Because Athaliah was not from the Southern Kingdom, but the North, Athaliah could not be God's choice.

But probably Satan was happy that Athaliah ruled. If Satan had a pawn, it was Athaliah. She set up a temple of Baal in the South, just as her mother Jezebel set up a temple for Baal in the North. Mattan, the priest of Baal, was employed to lead worship of Baal. But Athaliah was not just content to setting up an opposing religion; she cut off the house of God to worshippers. People could no longer bring their sheep to the Temple for sacrifice. Probably Athaliah's soldiers stopped them in the streets of Jerusalem, perhaps taking their sheep and sacrifice so the people could not express their repentance for sin and seek forgiveness from God.

But the worst thing that Athaliah did was a genocide against anyone who had the blood of David flowing in their veins. She killed all her grandsons, their cousins and any nephews that came from the godly line of Jehoshaphat. Why? "'Because' they said, 'he is the son of Jehoshaphat who sought the Lord with all his heart.' So the house of Ahaziah had no one to assume power over the kingdom" (2 Chron. 22:9).

Athaliah was neurotic over her power. She was accompanied by soldiers everywhere she went; first to protect her from those who resisted her reign, and second, to carry out her evil commands.

The evil blood of Jezebel poisoned the bloodstream of Athaliah. The curse was carried over into her son, Ahaziah. But something happened when her grandson, Joash, was conceived. Joash had a heart for God.

Why Did the Grandson Turn Out Good?

When Athaliah was scouring the Kingdom to kill any heir to the throne, somehow she overlooked a little one-year-old boy, Joash. Like King Herod, who slaughtered the children of Bethlehem to eliminate Jesus who was born "King of the Jews," Athaliah, a prototype a thousand years earlier, tried to kill any child that would be "King of the Jews."

The grandson had the influence of a good woman. Little Joash had a great aunt, i.e., Jehosheba, the actual sister of Athaliah. Somehow this good woman didn't have the evil heart of her sister, Athaliah. Great Aunt Jehosheba ran into the room, picked up a one-year-old baby boy—Joash—and dashed away to hide him in her room in the Temple.

As queen Athaliah scoured every apartment in the palace, looking for royal seed, she never realized the next king was hidden in the Temple. There was a wall of separation between the royal kings and the priestly men of God. The Bible says, "But Jehoshebe, the daughter of King Joram, sister of Ahaziah, took Joash the son of Ahaziah, and stole him away from among the king's sons who were being murdered; and they hid him and his nurse in the bedroom, from Athaliah, so that he was not killed" (2 Kings 11:2).

Why did Jehosheba do it? Was it her natural love for little babies? Could be! Was it her sibling rivalry against Athaliah? Could be! Did Jehosheba detest the evil her sister Athaliah did? Could be! Was it because Jehosheba had faith that young Joash could become the next king? Could be! Was it because Jehosheba knew that Messiah could come from the line of David, and she must make sure that the future Messiah was born? It could be all of the above reasons.

Joash had the influence of a godly environment. This young boy was reared in the Temple. What do you think he heard around the table as his great-aunt and great-uncle talked? He probably heard them talking about worship to God . . . and the forgiveness of sins . . . and the ministry of the Temple. Everything that this young impressionable child heard or saw was about God and service to God. Joash wasn't just hidden in the Temple, he was hidden with godly people in the Temple. "He [Joash] was hidden with them in the house of God for six years, while Athaliah reigned over the land" (2 Chron. 22:12).

Joash had the influence of a good grand-uncle. Jehoiada, the high priest and great-uncle, had a godly influence on young Joash's life. Jehoiada had great faith. When he finally revealed his secret—the presence of the child—to all the priests, he made a *faith-statement* that David's son would sit on the throne. "He [Jehoiada] said unto them, 'Behold, the king's son shall reign, as the LORD has said of the sons of David'" (2 Chron. 23:3).

Jehoiada was a man of principle. He not only had deep faith, he put his faith into action. He organized some of the Levites to guard young Joash with sword, spear and shield. He organized other priests to make a joyful announcement and celebration of his coronation. He organized still other priests for their duties in the great coronation of the young seven-year-old Joash. "So the Levites and all Judah did according to all that Jehoiada the priest commanded" (2 Chron. 23:8).

Joash had the influence of the regal coronation. Notice that Joash didn't sneak into the office. He was crowned as former kings were crowned. There wasn't a secret plot to assassinate Athaliah, nor did they wait for the queen's natural death. No, a great coronation was planned, the way a king should enter the office. "And they brought out the king's son, put the crown on him, gave him the Testimony, and made him king. Then Jehoiada and his sons anointed him, and said, 'Long live the king!'" (2 Chron. 23:11).

Can you see the great coronation? A seven-year-old boy wearing a royal red robe that is too long for him? He's wearing a crown that's too big for him, and he's going to assume an office that will overwhelm him. The young boy could never rule the nation without the godly influence of wise Jehoiada, the high priest who will become the power behind the throne.

The coronation was done in the right way, i.e., in public view. It was done at the right place, near the pillar in the Temple in God's house. It was done in the presence of all the people, so they cried out, "God save the king!" It was done with the right symbols of office, i.e., a king was anointed, he sat up on the throne, and the royal trumpets announced his coronation.

Joash was under the control of the sovereignty of God. Sometimes when people have done everything they can, they do not see that God's hand is in the small details. God controls big events in small ways, but nevertheless, God sovereignly controls. "Yet the Lord would not destroy the house of David, because of the covenant that He had made with David, and since He had promised to give a lamp to him and to his sons forever" (2 Chron. 21:7).

Joash was the only seed left in the line of David. If Athaliah had killed him, Satan would have succeeded. The genocide by Grandmother Athaliah was Satan's attempt to cut off the Messiah, before Jesus was ever born. Satan knew the promise that Messiah would crush his head so Satan wanted desperately to destroy the feet of Him who would be the "head crusher." But God preserved the life of a little boy who would be king, and because of that; one day Jesus the King will rule.

A Good Grandson

Joash made a pledge of devotion. Joash could have followed the influence of his evil father, but the spiritual high priest Jehoiada led the young king to make a promise to God and the people. Jehoiada made a covenant between himself, the people and the king, that they should be the Lord's people (see 2 Chron. 23:16).

What does a promise involve? That the people "shall love the LORD your God with all your heart, with all your soul, and with all your strength" (Deut. 6:5). Moses had taught obedience in the Torah, and now young Joash pledged his commitment to God. But a pledge to God also meant a separation from the world. God had said, "You shall have no other gods before Me" (Exod. 20:3), so Joash would have no room for other gods in his kingdom.

All the things that the young boy heard around the meal tables from his great-aunt and -uncle, he began to implement in his rule. God would be first in the kingdom, and in individual lives. God would be worshipped in the Temple, and the people could bring their sacrifices. The land would be purged of idols, and God's people would obey the Law.

Joash cleansed the land of sin. Because Joash had pledged his devotion to God, the land had to be cleansed of sin. "And all the people went to the temple of Baal, and tore it down. They broke in pieces its altars and images, and killed Mattan the priest of Baal before the altars" (2 Chron. 23:17). The people "took no prisoners"; isn't it what Athaliah did against the godly seed in the family? She killed them all. When the enemy is *absolutely evil,* why is it that critics complain when reformers are *absolutely just?*

Joash re-instituted worship. The people had not been able to bring their sacrifices into the Temple of the Lord. Perhaps the soldiers of Athaliah had been stationed in front of the Temple to prohibit people from entering with sacrifices. Perhaps it was just intimidation? Perhaps it was fear of reprisals or weakness on the part of the people?

Whatever the reason, when Joash became king, the people were commanded to bring their sacrifices to God, and worship Him. "Also Jehoiada appointed the oversight of the house of the LORD to the hand of the priests, the Levites, whom David had assigned in the house of the LORD, to offer the burnt offerings of the LORD, as [it is] written in the Law of Moses, with rejoicing and with singing, [as it was established] by David" (2 Chron. 23:18). The Temple worship that had ceased was re-established.

But just don't look at the re-establishment of religious tradition, or look to see obedience on the part of the people. When the sacrifices were brought, the people repented of their sins, and God forgave them. The people were reunited to God in fellowship and obedience. And a people who know their God and live in fellowship with Him can do exploits for God. When Joash reestablished worship, he strengthened the people and the kingdom.

Joash enforced discipline. Not only did Joash make the house of God to be holy and effective, he also didn't want unclean people entering the Temple. When Athaliah ruled the nation, apparently she could enter the Temple any time that she wanted. Her wicked heart and bloody hands polluted the Temple when she walked unhindered in the house of God. But young Joash decided: enough was enough! "And he set the gatekeepers at the gates of the house of the LORD, so that no one [who was] in any way unclean should enter" (2 Chron. 23:19). If the house of God was to be holy, Joash made sure that only those who were spiritually clean could enter God's house.

Joash was loyal to the symbols of the office. God loves symbols, whether it's the symbols of the Lord's Table, i.e., the broken bread symbolizing the body of Jesus and the cup symbolizing the spilled blood; or whether it's the cross symbolizing Jesus' death, or whether it's baptism to symbolize our identification with Jesus with His death and resurrection.

So God was pleased when the symbols of office were followed as young Joash was crowned king. He was anointed with oil, symbolic of the Holy Spirit coming in his life. He was given the Testimonies, i.e., the Word of God, symbolic of the righteous judgments by which the nation would be ruled. He sat upon the throne of the kingdom that was symbolic of its power. He was crowned in the house of God, recognizing the presence of God. And where did he learn about the symbols? He learned them from Great-Uncle Jehoiada, the high priest, who understood God gave the symbols their meaning.

Joash had a good testimony to the kingdom. As long as Great-Uncle Jehoiada was an influence in his life, "Joash did [what was] right in the sight of the LORD all the days of Jehoiada the priest" (2 Chron. 24:2).

How to Raise Godly Grandchildren

Make sure grandchildren are protected from the Evil One. It is possible that a godly relative can offset the influence of an ungodly parent or grandparent. So, in your family if there is an ungodly influence on children, you can make a positive difference. Determine to imitate the godly influence of Jehoiada and Jehosheba. Ask God to help you influence a child for godliness.

Raise children in a godly environment. The commitment of King Joash to the house of God can be measured by his early life in the house of God. Perhaps he destroyed the house of Baal because he had a love for the house of God. So, make sure your grandchildren are taken to Sunday school and the house of God. If your church has programs such as Boys' Brigade, AWANA, Training Union or youth activities, make sure your grandchildren are there. Your grandchildren need the godly influence of a good home environment. If they don't have it in the home of their mother and father, make sure they have it when they come to see you. Make sure there is Christian music, Christian symbols on the wall, and Christian books out in prominent places. Give them Christian records, a Bible, and other things that will influence their lives.

A child needs many godly resources to influence his life for godliness. A godly mother and father cannot do it alone in our "perilous times" (2 Tim. 3:1). The ungodly influence of music, television, movies, and our entire environment works against your grandchildren. How can your grandchildren be godly when they see so much rebellion, crime, drugs, cursing and illicit sex on the media? Your grandchild needs the influence of a godly church and if possible, a godly Christian school. The grandchild needs role models at church, as well as godly examples of parents and, grandparents. The grandchild need compliments from godly people, as well as support at church activities, camp, ministry opportunities and mission trips. It's going to take as many resources as possible to make your grandchildren godly and to keep them from evil.

Celebrate the significant passages of life in a godly way. One of the reasons Joash remained strong for so long was the events that happened on the day of his coronation. It was not just the positive things that were done, i.e., the robe, the crown, trumpets and the shouts of the people, "God save the king!" It was not just the anointing, the Testimony and sitting on the throne. Young Joash would have remembered hearing his grandmother scream in the Temple, "TREASON!" He would have remembered the command of his great-uncle Jehoiada to not kill her in the Temple, but to take her out to the stables to kill her. This was probably one of those negative messages that made an indelible imprint on his mind.

And what are the passages that will influence your grandchildren? Is it their baby dedication at church, even though they don't remember it? (You should remind them.) Is it when you dedicated them to God in your living room? Is it when they graduated from kindergarten and you were there? Was it on special Grandparents Day when you were there? How about the times that they participated in a Christmas play at church, or a sports event, did you cheer? What about the graduation from grade school . . . junior high . . . high school . . . and college? All these passages are important, and your support will point them in the right direction.

Get rid of evil forces from a grandchild's life. While parents are responsible for much of the environment in your grandchildren's life, you can have an influence for godliness. Do as much as possible to get rid of the influence of ungodly television, such as explicit sex, drug use, lawlessness, demon worship, and don't let your grandchildren make heroes and heroines of ungodly media models.

What does that mean to you? Get rid of alcohol in your refrigerator; how can you ask them to refrain from drunkenness when your refrigerator evidences first tastes toward drunkenness? Get rid of channels on your television that provide explicit sex, i.e., movie channels. How can you influence them to be holy when they may take their first visual step across the lines of innocence watching your television? Get rid of books and magazines where they might peek. A filthy picture is like a little black ink in a glass of water; it is no longer pure.

Help your grandchild make decisions and use your influence to help keep them from bad decisions. Life is choice and when you help grandchildren make good choices, you help them to live good lives. Remember, you can't tell them what to do, but you can point them in the right direction. You can point them away from the consequences of evil decisions. You can point out the long-term advantages of good decisions. Children don't think in the future tense; all they see is what's in the world about them. But grandparents think by the "big picture." So use your "big view of life" to influence and help them see a larger picture of their life.

When grandchildren don't have discipline, give them an environment where they do the right thing and they can develop self-discipline. It is very difficult for grandparents to have undisciplined children around. However, you can't keep them from coming into your home just because they are hyperactive, or they won't obey you. However, you can create an environment where they do the right thing. Remember, you're older than children, you're smarter than children, and you are tougher (emotionally) than children. Use your *lifepurpose* to point children in the right direction. Get them doing what you want them to do. Don't emphasize the negative, i.e., what they shouldn't do, give them an environment where they will do the right thing. Help them develop self-discipline to do the right thing.

Remember, the power of an example is great, therefore before you can teach self-discipline to a child; you must have self-discipline. Therefore, grandparents must know who they are, what they should do for God, and how to get it done. With that confidence, grandparents can teach grandchildren who they are, what God wants them to do, and how they can do God's will.

7

Mephibosheth:
Grandson of King Saul

Living Below Your Inheritance

GRANDFATHER, SAUL—DISOBEYED GOD
SON, JONATHAN—GODLY
GRANDSON, MEPHIBOSHETH—NEEDED HIS INHERITANCE

*"Now when Mephibosheth the son of Jonathan, the son of Saul, had come
to David, he fell on his face and prostrated himself. Then David said,
'Mephibosheth?' And he answered, 'Here is your servant!' So David said to him,
'Do not fear, for I will surely show you kindness for Jonathan your father's sake,
and will restore to you all the land of Saul your grandfather; and you shall eat
bread at my table continually.' Then he bowed himself, and said, 'What is your
servant, that you should look upon such a dead dog as I?'"*

2 SAMUEL 9:6-8

My name is Mephibosheth; I know it's a hard name to say but my name means "desolation." And "desolation" surely describes my life.

I am a cripple, and most people think a cripple can't do much. They may be right. If a cripple owns a farm, he can't work the fields. If a cripple works in town, he's got to have legs to get around. When you're crippled, you end up poor with no money . . . no friends . . . no one invites you to their house to eat . . . crippled boys have a desolate life.

I wasn't born crippled. When word came that my grandfather Saul and father Jonathan had been killed, everyone was afraid the Philistines were coming to kill me too. So, a servant girl picked me up to run away . . . and then there was a terrible accident. I don't blame her. She was trying to save me, but my legs were mangled for life.

I said no one invited me to eat at their house; there may be another reason than being a cripple. I am the grandson of Saul; you know, King Saul who tried to kill David. Today, everyone loves David, so they are afraid to be nice to me. My grandfather Saul was so jealous he tried to kill David . . . again . . . and again . . . and again. Because people haven't gotten over that, they shun me, simply because I am the grandson of Saul.

Then I got word that David wanted to see me. At first, I thought David might want to put me in prison to make sure I didn't start an uprising or even kill me. How was I to know that David was such a gracious man? Rather than killing me because I was the grandson of Saul, David wanted to take care of me and restore unto me my grandfather's farm.

Let me tell you how wonderful King David is. First, he restored to me my grandfather's farm, and I now own it and my sons live there. Also, my father had a servant named Ziba. David told Ziba to work the farm and give the food to my sons.

Remember, I told you that nobody wanted me to eat at their house because they hated Saul. Well today, I eat all my meals at the table with King David. Can you imagine that? An outcast is a friend of the king. I live in the palace with the king, I get to see the king every day, and I eat with the king. Isn't that grace? That's a picture of how God takes care of us. We once were an outcast, but now the King of kings has given us everything.

Why Mephibosheth Lived Below His Inheritance

Lesson to Take Away

When grandchildren live below the benefits of their spiritual inheritance, grandparents can help them reach the level of their spiritual potential.

Mephibosheth was the grandson of a king, yet he lived as an indigent, i.e., a street person. He was not welcomed in anyone's home; he did not have a job. He lived far below his inheritance. A family named Mechir took care of his basic necessaries. Even though Mephibosheth may have known that he was a grandson of a king, he did not live up to his inheritance, nor did he know how to take advantage of his inheritance.

Physical Problems. Mephibosheth was not as strong as his father, Jonathan. His grandfather Saul had a massive physical physique; he stood head and shoulders above the average man. But not Mephibosheth. He was probably ridiculed by other children when growing up because children can be cruel to one another. "Jonathan . . . had a son that was lame in his feet. He was five-years-old when tidings came [a father and grandfather's death] and his nurse picked him up and fled: And it happened, as she made haste to flee, that he fell and became lame" (2 Sam. 4:4).

What Can We Assume About Mephibosheth's Problem?

- He became crippled in an accident.
- Not one foot, but both feet.
- The accident kept him from physical activities.

- The accident kept him from growing physically strong.
- Being crippled produced negative self-perception.

There is no mention how the accident happened. Did he fall under a moving wagon? Some galloping horses? Down the stairs? There is no indication in the text that Mephibosheth blamed the nurse for the accident, or for being crippled. All he knew that he was lame in both feet and could not walk; he was a cripple for life.

Name Problems. Not only was he crippled and could not live a normal life, Mephibosheth's name means "shame that destroys." When Mephibosheth was born, he was given the name Meribaal (1 Chron. 8:34), which meant "Baal fighter." Was this a name given by his godly father Jonathan that meant the young boy would fight Baal? Was this a name given by his grandfather Saul, who later in his life turned away from Jehovah, so he named his grandson "fighter for Baal"? In any case, after the accident the lad was given a second name, i.e., Mephibosheth, "shame that destroys." People were ashamed of the little boy with crippled feet and their reaction destroyed his self-esteem.

Heritage problems. Mephibosheth's grandfather had disobeyed God, tried to kill David, and even visited an evil witch. Because the people knew that Saul's disobedience brought hardship to the nation, they rejected Saul, and refused any reference to his reign. That meant that they rejected Mephibosheth. Young Mephibosheth couldn't claim a kingly inheritance because the people were ashamed of his grandfather Saul.

Geographical problems. Mephibosheth ended up living outside the Promised Land, east across the Jordan River in Lodebar (a name that means "no pasture"). He was living up in the hills of the nation we know today as Jordan. Not only was he living "out of the way," he was living out of the land that God had promised to bless.

Living Less Than Christian

Ignoring our new position. Many Christians, like Mephibosheth, cannot follow Christ or His disciples because they are crippled by sin. Many Christians are strangers in this sinful world, "begging" to make ends meet. But children of God should recognize where they are "in Christ." They should notice what God has done for them, "Made us alive together with Christ . . . raised us up together . . . and made us sit together in heavenly places in Christ Jesus" (Eph. 2:5-6). Every Christian has a new position in Christ, has been raised spiritually from the dead, has been seated with Jesus Christ in the heavenlies; so why do they live like a beggar? Like Mephibosheth, many Christians are living below their inheritance. Are your grandchildren living below their spiritual inheritance?

You do not enjoy heavenly things. If you know Jesus Christ, you are a child of the heavenly Father. "But as many as received Him, to them He gave the right to become children of God" (John 1:12) And what does the Father do to His children? He gives them spiritual blessings: "(Jesus Christ) has blessed us with every spiritual blessing in the heavenly places in Christ" (Eph. 1:3).

You are obsessed with temptations. Too often Christians focus on their problems and temptations rather than their position in Christ, "seated next to God the Father in heaven." Quit looking at sin and its attractiveness. Quit focusing on your fleshly desires to sin because that will bring defeat. Paul testified of his weakness to temptation when he said, "For the good that I will to do, I do not do; but the evil I will not to do, that I practice" (Rom. 7:19).

You are defeated. When you always focus on temptation, you eventually give in to temptation. Many Christians are defeated because they always think about temptation, rather than thinking about their new heavenly position in Christ Jesus. Paul tells us we can have victory: "thanks be to God who always leads us in triumph in Christ" (2 Cor. 2:14).

A Cripple Elevated

By the work of another. If you are a spiritual cripple, you will be elevated by the work of Jesus Christ, not by your own work. David took an initiative to change Mephibosheth's life. David said, "Is there still anyone who is left of the house of Saul, that I may show him kindness for Jonathan's sake?" (2 Sam. 9:1). David and Jonathan were friends. Even though Jonathan had the right to the throne because he was Saul's son, Jonathan gave up his "rights" for David. He gave up his royal robe because he knew that David was God's man for the throne. In the same way, Jesus gave up his "right" for us. "Christ Jesus . . . being in the form of God . . . taking the form of the servant, and coming in the likeness of man" (Phil. 2:5-7).

God uses people. David did not know about Mephibosheth, or any other child of King Saul. When David asked if there were any of Saul's grandchildren left, God used Ziba to change the life of Mephibosheth. When David asked the question—probably to his entire court—Ziba said unto the king, "There is still a son of Jonathan who is lame in his feet" (2 Sam. 9:3). God uses other people to make a difference in our life. Sometimes God uses parents . . . a friend . . . or a grandparent. If Ziba had not spoken up, Mephibosheth would have remained a beggar in Lodebara.

Gratitude is the least remembered of all virtues,
and the acid test of your character.

Right Motivation. David did not show kindness to Mephibosheth for his own reputation, nor did David plan to get anything out of Mephibosheth. David remembered all that Jonathan had sacrificed for him, so David wanted to return the kindness. King David told his court that he would bring Mephibosheth to his table, "That I may show the kindness of God to him" (2 Sam. 9:3).

How to Claim an Inheritance

Realize that you are not worthy. None of us is worthy of the blessings of God; God's grace always takes the initiative. When Mephibosheth finally entered the court of King David, he only had one response: "Behold, your servant" (2 Sam. 7:6). Likewise, we do not come into the presence of God in our own good works, nor our own righteousness. What must we say? "We are unprofitable servants. We have done what was our duty to do" (Luke 17:10).

Recognize you are dead. When Mephibosheth was brought into the court of David, he did not remind the king of his royal blood, nor did he demand his inheritance. What was Mephibosheth's attitude? "And he bowed himself and said . . . that thou shall look upon a dead dog" (2 Sam. 9:8). Mephibosheth knew that he was nothing, had nothing, and could become nothing. Mephibosheth knew that grace had brought him into the king's court.

If God has given us a spiritual meal,
why are we living with only a few crumbs?

Realize that all things are yours. Mephibosheth was the son of a king, but he did not act like a king. It was said that David said to him, "I have given you . . . all that pertaineth to Saul and to all his house" (2 Sam. 9:9). Suddenly with the words of the king, Mephibosheth was made a wealthy man.

We have nothing in this world, but the Word of God makes us spiritually wealthy. God has given us all spiritual things. "If then you are raised with Christ, seek those things which are above" (Col. 3:1). Since we are children of God, we should not focus on this world, but set our aim to live for God according to all He provides: "Set your aim on things above, not on things on this earth" (Col. 3:2).

Appropriate daily food. Because of the words of the king, Mephibosheth did not have to worry about anything else. King David said, "Mephibosheth . . . shall eat at my table" (2 Sam. 9:11). Mephibosheth didn't have another worry. Whether the servants liked him or not, they had to serve a meal to Mephibosheth. Whether the cooks liked it or not, they prepared a meal for Mephibosheth. Because the king had spoken, Mephibosheth didn't have to worry about anything.

God has given us biblical promises. The Lord is our King and has spoken. So why do you worry? What does the Bible say? "My God shall supply all your need" (Phil. 4:19). But we have so many frustrations. We want so many things that we shouldn't desire. When we set our focus on Jesus Christ, we will only desire those things that He will give us: "Delight yourself also in the Lord, that He shall give you the desires of your heart" (Ps. 37:4).

Claim help from the Helper. Mephibosheth was given the property, Saul's farm. But he was crippled. There was no way he could work his fields and take advantage of his assets. King David turned to Ziba and said, "You Ziba and your sons and your servants shall work the land for Mephibosheth to bring the harvest that Mephibosheth' sons will have to eat" (2 Sam. 9:10). From that day on, Ziba would be servant to Mephibosheth, and Saul's farm would be worked by Ziba and his sons. Mephibosheth didn't need the food from the farm because he was eating at the king's table. But Mephibosheth had sons; they were members of Saul's family. Actually, they were Saul's great-grandsons. Ziba was to work the farm so the sons could eat. Notice, Mephibosheth didn't have to worry for himself or for his children.

God has promised to take care of you. The night before Jesus died, He promised, "I will pray the Father, and He will give you another helper" (John 14:16). That helper is the Holy Spirit. We have heard the Holy Spirit called "the Comforter," which is the name translated in the *Old King James Bible*. But the translation "helper" gives us a better understanding of how the Holy Spirit ministers to us. We are the sons of the King and the Holy Spirit will help us claim our inheritance.

Enjoy the King's presence. Not only was Mephibosheth's daily needs satisfied, he could have daily fellowship with the king. "Mephibosheth dwelt in Jerusalem for he ate continually at the king's table" (2 Sam. 9:13). Who eats at the king's table? The sons of the king, as well as his friends and court. Therefore, Mephibosheth was able to live up to his inheritance, and because he had royal blood flowing in his veins, he was able to eat daily at the king's table.

You are a child of God, therefore you can have daily fellowship with the Lord. Long before David became king he said as a shepherd boy, "That I may dwell in the house of the Lord forever" (Ps. 23:6). It wasn't the house that David was interested in; it was the presence of God who dwelt over the Ark of the Covenant. When David looked up and saw that blue flame—the Shekinah-glory cloud—he knew that God was in the house. So what did David do? He worshiped the Lord. And another place David expressed the same desire to fellowship with God, "That I may dwell in the house of the Lord all the days of my life, to behold the beauty of the Lord" (Ps. 27:4).

Grandchildren must change their thinking about their inheritance, before they can enjoy the benefits of the inheritance. So you pray that they may understand what God has done for them. You want them to change their thinking, so they will change their actions. Your grandchildren must claim the benefits that are theirs. You cannot do it for them; all you can do is offer them your love and support; they must respond and they must repent of sin. When your hand is held out to them, they must take it. Your grandchildren can benefit from you, even after your death. Even though godly Jonathan was dead, Mephibosheth benefited long after Jonathan was gone. In the same way, you want your grandchildren to benefit spiritually long after you are gone.

8

Joel:

Grandson of Hannah

When Grandchildren Are Pushed into Ministry

GRANDMOTHER—HANNAH
SON—SAMUEL
GRANDSONS—JOEL AND ABIAH

"Now it came to pass when Samuel was old that he made his sons judges over Israel. The name of his firstborn was Joel, and the name of his second, Abijah; they were judges in Beersheba. But his sons did not walk in his ways; they turned aside after dishonest gain, took bribes, and perverted justice. Then all the elders of Israel gathered together and came to Samuel at Ramah, and said to him, Look, you are old, and your sons do not walk in your ways. Now make us a king to judge us like all the nations."

1 SAMUEL 8:1-5

My name is Joel; I am the grandson to Hannah. She is my grandmother who prayed to God to give her a son. That son was my father Samuel. I am the son of Samuel. My father was a priest. Since all priests come from the tribe of Levi, my father's family, I was destined to become a priest.

It's not easy being the son of a famous man. My father Samuel heard the voice of God speak to him late one night in the Tabernacle. Everyone follows my father Samuel because they know that God speaks to him. I've never heard God's voice.

My father Samuel was responsible for the great spiritual revival and the great battle that defeated the Philistines. When my father gathered all the people together at Ramah, the Spirit of God came upon the people. When the Philistines attacked him, my father Samuel prayed and God sent a great thunderstorm that helped defeat the Philistines. I've never won a great battle.

When I was a boy growing up, everyone was nice to me because of my father. I had special meals, and special privileges, all because people loved my father Samuel.

Growing up I never wanted to be a warrior judge like Jephthah . . . or lead soldiers into battle like the judge Gideon; I didn't think I could do that. But my father Samuel made me a judge anyway.

He sent me to Beersheba—my first place of ministry. The people were demanding and I didn't want to work that hard. I told them if they wanted me to help them, they would have to pay me more. They did! I found that I could make a lot of money by charging for my services, and the people paid.

When the people sinned, they needed me to offer a blood sacrifice for them, and they paid me. Because the people sinned a lot, I made a lot of money.

Then I decided to keep taking their money, but not offer the blood sacrifice. They'd never know . . . no one would know, except me.

After a while, I just got lazy. I stopped offering sacrifices altogether. Then I stopped obeying the Sabbath law, and before you knew it, I'd broken several other laws. It was then that the people complained to my father Samuel.

There is an end to this story. My father dealt with me severely; he remembered how the priest before him—Eli—was punished for not dealing severely with his sons. So, my father straightened me out. Years later as my father faced death, he was proud of me and announced it to all of Israel. And all the elders of Israel agreed with him. I'm glad for a good father who made me do right.

A Godly Grandmother

Lesson to Take Away

Grandparents should not "force" or put pressure on their grandchildren to go into ministry because there are severe problems for those who enter the ministry but are not called of God.

Grandmother Hannah was a godly woman and if she had not prayed and fasted, her son Samuel would not have been a great man of God, nor would there have been the grandsons Joel and Abiah. But God raised up Samuel, called the greatest of the judges, because Hannah was a godly grandmother. But what happened to his sons Joel and Abiah?

God raised up judges. Throughout the book of Judges, God always raised up a deliverer when the people repented of sin and called on the Lord. First, God's people fell into sin. Second, God allowed the heathen nations to oppress Israel and put them in servitude. Then God's people repented and cried out for deliverance. It was then that God raised up a judge who delivered them. Notice with each cycle, "The Lord raised up judges which delivered them" (Judg. 2:16). A man didn't decide to become a judge; God raised him up. Therefore, we can conclude that surely a parent didn't put their children into ministry.

Joel and Abiah weren't raised up by God. Obviously God raised up Samuel to deliver Israel from her oppressors, and to lead the nation into its first great revival. Just as all great men face death, so when Samuel was sixty years old, he began to think about dying. Who would take his place? His first thought was his sons. "When Samuel was old that he made his sons judges over Israel" (1 Sam. 8:1).

There's nothing wrong with a man of God wanting his sons to enter the ministry. That's a natural desire for most every minister of God. Howbeit, everyone must recognize that young people enter the ministry because of the "call of God," not the desire of their parents. When Samuel made his sons judges, some have asked if he did not wrongly push his children into ministry.

Why Samuel may have been right to appoint his sons. Because we were not there, we didn't see all of the conditions. We may not understand why Samuel appointed his sons to ministry. Samuel may have done the right thing. However, God raised up a judge in response to a crisis; but there was no crisis facing Israel when Samuel put his sons in office. Also, God uses humans to carry out His will. On many occasions God used a father to introduce his son into leadership, such as David prepared Solomon to be king after him. So what's wrong with Samuel preparing his sons to be judge after him?

Then again, remember that Grandmother Hannah sent young Samuel to minister in the Tabernacle when he was but a young child. When most young boys go into elementary school, Hannah left Samuel at the Tabernacle, and he stayed there the rest of his life. So isn't it natural that Hannah's son Samuel would do the same thing to his sons? Samuel was just doing to his sons what his mother did to him.

Why Samuel may have been wrong. Even though Samuel's motives may have been pure, there may be other reasons why he acted independently of God's will. Perhaps at age sixty Samuel thought he was going to die, or perhaps he prematurely wanted to retire. What Samuel didn't know was that he would live another thirty-eight years, i.e., he wouldn't die until he was ninety-eight years old. Men of God should be careful not to prematurely "retire" or leave the ministry for which they are trained. After all when you get to be a "senior saint" you know more, have experienced more, and are able to accomplish more in your ministry than any other time in your life. Why quit?

Also, Samuel should have remembered the negative example of Eli and his sons. God spoke to Samuel when he was child with a message of judgment for Eli. The old judge Eli was punished by God because he didn't correct his disobedient sons. Shouldn't Samuel have seen the same disobedience in his own son? Shouldn't Samuel have recognized that God would judge him for the sins of his sons, just as He judged Eli?

When the Bible says that "His [Samuel] sons walked not in his ways" (1 Sam. 8:3), the older father should have known better than put them in ministry. The people rejected the sons, "The elders . . . said to him [Samuel] . . . your sons do not walk in your ways" (1 Sam. 8:4, 5). When Samuel was rebuked, he reacted to the elders, just as any modern-day father reacts when people criticize his son. "The thing displeased Samuel when they said, Give us a king to judge us" (1 Sam. 8:6).

If Samuel was wrong in putting his sons into office, it had long-range political consequences. The people prematurely began begging for a king, and the office of the king was prematurely instituted in Israel. "The elders said . . . Give us a king to judge us" (1 Sam. 8:4-6).

Grandmother Hannah was an extraordinary woman. She obeyed God, and each year went up to the Tabernacle to worship the Lord. But she was more than just another godly woman. She was an extraordinary woman who believed in prayer and fasting. When faced with her childlessness, "She (Hannah) wept and did not eat . . . she prayed unto the Lord and wept" (1 Sam. 1:7, 10). The Bible indicates that she did more than pray once; she prayed continually for a son. She had such deep faith in God that she prayed until she got an answer.

Grandmother Hannah was single focused. Hannah's entire focus in life was on serving God and walking with Him. When Eli the old priest thought she was drunk in the Tabernacle, she said, denying, "I am not drunk," then she explained, "for out of the abundance of my complaint and grief I have spoken until now" (1 Sam. 1:16). Hannah described what she did: "[She] poured out her soul to God." It was a description of the depth of her prayers.

Grandmother Hannah dedicated her child to God. The greatest thing that God had given her in her life, she dedicated back to God. "Now I am giving him to the Lord, and he will belong to the Lord his whole life" (1 Sam. 1:28). Since God had been so good to give her a child—the name Samuel means to ask—she gave him back to the Lord.

Grandmother Hannah worshipped the Lord. When God answered her prayer, Hannah did more than say *AMEN*: she composed an entire Psalm to God (see 1 Sam. 2). "My heart rejoices in the Lord" (1 Sam. 2:1).

Samuel Faithfully Served the Lord

Samuel faithfully served the Lord all of his life. Even while a small child, "The boy Samuel ministered to the Lord before Eli" (1 Sam. 3:1). Samuel even did small tasks well, such as making sure the lamp in the Tabernacle didn't go out: "Samuel laid down to sleep next to the Ark of God so that the lamp did not go out in the Temple at night" (1 Sam. 3:3, author's translation).

Samuel talked with God. Because Samuel was faithful in all things, God trusted him and talked with him. Three times in one evening, the young child Samuel heard his named being called. Each time Samuel responded, "Here am I" (1 Sam. 3:1, 6, 8). When old Eli instructed young Samuel to say, "Speak, Lord, for Your servant hears" (1 Sam. 3:9), it was then that God spoke to Samuel. "Now the Lord came and stood . . . then the Lord said to Samuel: Behold, I will do something in Israel" (1 Sam. 3:10, 11).

Samuel ministered for a lifetime. Some people serve the Lord faithfully for a while, and other people serve the Lord with great zeal for a longer time. "But Samuel judged Israel all the days of his life" (1 Sam. 7:15).

What the Prodigal Grandsons Did Wrong

The prodigal grandsons rejected their father's attitude and actions. Sometimes grandchildren just don't want to be like their grandfather. Sometimes a prodigal grandson will reject a grandfather's Christian ways, saying, "He's a stick in the mud," or "He's not cool." The grandsons did not follow the godliness of Hannah, nor did they follow the lifestyle of their father: "But his sons did not walk in his ways" (1 Sam. 8:3). When you think of walking, first of all, walking involves a destination. The sons decided not to walk toward the goal of their father. Second, walking involves style and attitude; the grandsons determined not to do it the way their father did it. And finally, walking involves effort and energy, and the grandsons determined not to put their strength in serving the things their father served.

The prodigal grandsons served for money. Perhaps Samuel was blinded to the real passion of his sons. If so, we can overlook Samuel's love for his children. However, if Samuel put them in office knowing their weakness, we cannot overlook his compromise. The sons "turned aside after dishonest gain" (1 Sam. 8:3).

It's wrong when anyone goes into the ministry for a salary, ease, or financial benefits. It's wrong when a minister is just concerned about a "40 hour week" or keeping his job.

The prodigal grandsons sold out to money. If a person enters the ministry for money, then money becomes the basis by which their decisions are made. When a person's goal in ministry is money, then he will do anything for money. Samuel's sons "took bribes" (1 Sam. 8:3). Perhaps they didn't take bribes to do something il- legal;perhaps they took bribes just because people offered them money. Sometimes people offer gifts and privileges to ministers to show their appreciation for what God has done for them. But any time that a person's gift gets them extra attention and privilege, the gift has become a bribe.

The prodigal grandsons violated the law. So the sons of Solomon did more than just accept money, they "perverted justice" (1 Sam. 8:3). This means they broke the law for money.

> When money is your primary goal,
> you will do anything to get money.

How to Train Children About Money

Teach them stewardship. Stewardship is not teaching children to give money to God, nor is it teaching children to be stingy. Stew- ardship is defined as *the proper management of time, talent, and trea- sure for the glory of God.* Therefore, both grandparents and parents should teach their children how to properly manage their money for the glory of God. Remember Paul's exhortation, "Moreover, stewards must faithfully manage everything for God" (1 Cor. 4:2, author's translation).

Teach grandchildren that money gain is not godliness. Too often peo- ple measure their success in life by the money that they make. Even in ministry, some people measure the success of their service to God by the church's budget. At other times, a minister might be judged by how much money he makes. But this is contrary to God's standards. Notice what Paul said: "False teachers think . . . that financial gain is godliness" (1 Tim. 6:3, 5, author's translation).

Therefore, what is great gain? Paul again answered that question: "Godliness that is satisfied with what you have is great gain" (1 Tim. 6:6, author's translation).

Teach grandchildren that lust for money will destroy them. When making money becomes more important than anything else in life, ultimately that passion for money will destroy the moneymaker. Greed is a hard taskmaster. "For the love of money is a root of all kinds of evil, for which some have strayed from the faith in their greediness, and pierced themselves through with many sorrows" (1 Tim. 6:10).

Teach grandchildren about Christian convictions. When you teach children the convictions of Jesus Christ, they will be balanced in all things. Notice again what Paul said: "But you, O man of God, flee these things and pursue righteousness, godliness, faith, love, patience, gentleness" (1 Tim. 6:11).

Teach grandchildren to use money properly. Money is a great tool: when used properly it can benefit the work of God, as well as yourself. However, don't love the tool, but rather love what God can do with the tool. No sculptor loves his hammer and chisel, but rather he loves the work of art that he can create. So with money, you can create a great work of art, i.e., you can influence lives. You can create a successful life, great churches, missionary projects, and the advancement of the kingdom of God.

Money is a tool to be used, so use it wisely. Notice what Jesus said about the man who had money but used it unwisely: "But he who had received one went and dug in the ground, and hid his lord's money" (Matt. 25:18). There are some misers who think it is wonderful to have a lot of money hidden in the ground, or in a bank account. What happens to the person whose only goal in life is to accumulate money? "But his lord answered and said to him, You wicked and lazy servant, you knew that I reap where I have not sown, and gather where I have not scattered seed. So you ought to have deposited my money with the bankers, and at my coming I would have received back my own with interest. So take the talent from him, and give it to him who has ten talents. For to everyone who has, more will be given, and he will have abundance; but from him who does not have, even what he has will be taken away" (Matt. 28:26-29).

9

Artaxerxes:

Grandson of Mordecai

Being Used of God in Unseen Ways

ADOPTED GRANDPA—MORDECAI
MOTHER—ESTHER
FATHER—AHASURUS (XERXES)
GRANDSON—ARTAXERXES

"There was a certain Jew whose name was Mordecai the son of . . .
Kish, a Benjamite. And Mordecai had brought up Hadassah, that is, Esther,
his uncle's daughter, for she had neither father nor mother. The young woman
was lovely and beautiful. When her father and mother died, Mordecai took
her as his own daughter."

ESTHER 2:5, 7

M y name is King Artaxerxes of Persia. I am the son of Xerxes, the prefix "arta" means "son of." I am king of Persia, the most powerful nation in the Near Eastern world. The Greeks are very powerful in the Western world and one day there will be a clash between the East and West, but that's not for me to talk about now.

I have a secret that not many people know about, and I don't tell many about it. It's not that I am ashamed of my secret; it's just that there are forces in my empire that could use my secret against me. There are forces in my empire that hate the Jewish people. The Jews are a small minority group of people from the land they call the Promised Land. I am half Jewish.

My mother Esther was a Jew who married my father Xerxes in about 478 BC. Even then very few people knew that she was a Jew, because the same forces that would oppose me would have used that same knowledge against her.

Let me tell you about my grandfather Mordecai. He's the one who adopted my mother Esther. So, I call him Grandpa Mordecai, even though he's not my biological grandfather.

Let me tell you how my father married my mother. My father Xerxes got mad at his first wife and divorced her. To find a second wife, he held a beauty pageant throughout the entire Persian kingdom to marry the most beautiful woman and make her queen. My mother Esther was gorgeous, she was gracious, she was elegant and she pleased my father, Xerxes. Before Esther became queen, Mordecai, her adopted father, told her not to tell anyone she was a Jew, because there were people in the kingdom who would use that information against her.

I am not going to tell you the whole story how a wicked prime minister tried to kill every Jew in the world. It was my mother Esther who saved the Jews. That's when my father, Xerxes, found out that she was a Jew. But it didn't make any difference to him. So, you need to know, I've got Jewish blood running in my veins.

I remember my mother's stories about Jerusalem . . . about Solomon's Temple . . . about the godly heroes of faith . . . David, Gideon,

Moses and Abraham. Mother said that God would also use me, but I didn't realize how He would use me, until one day I got my chance.

I had a cupbearer named Nehemiah who sat next to me in all my meals. He protected me from being poisoned; he was a member of my personal guard. I trusted him because he was Jewish and he knew my secret.

One particular day, Nehemiah was really sad; I could see it in his face. Even when he forced a smile, it did not come from his heart. When I asked him what was wrong, he said, "The city of Jerusalem is desolate, the walls are destroyed, and the surrounding nations laugh at the Jews."

Out of that conversation I saw my chance to do something for God, to help reestablish God's eternal city—Jerusalem. I gave Nehemiah a letter authorizing him to go back to build the walls of Jerusalem. I gave him a letter of credit to get all the money he needed to get the job done.

When Nehemiah finishes building those walls, people won't remember what I did. I won't tell them what I did because I don't want them to know that I am half Jewish. The people will give all the credit to Nehemiah, and that's all right; but I'll know that I had a part in preparing for the coming King who will rule over all the earth. Did you hear what I said? There is coming a Jewish King; He'll have 100 percent Jewish blood in His veins, and He'll rule the entire earth, and I'll be glad to bow at His feet and worship Him.

What Is Known About the Family

Lesson to Take Away

When you are in a situation where you can't tell everyone you're a Christian and you can't ever share your faith, God can use you in a great way, just as He used Esther and her son, Artaxerxes.

Royal blood. We all know that Esther became queen of Persia, but most forget that royal blood flowed in her veins long before she was providentially crowned queen of the most powerful empire on earth. She was a cousin to Mordecai . . . the son of Kish (the line of Saul, first king of Israel) (Est. 2:5). As an impoverished girl growing up in the Persian Empire, what did she know about her ancestor the prestigious King Saul? Sometimes a small child's self-perception prepares them for their station in life. Could Esther's "royal self-perception" have prepared her to be Queen Esther over Persia?

Orphaned. We don't know anything about Esther's home life. As a matter of fact, all we know is that "her father and mother were dead" (Est. 2:7). We don't know if they were rich, if they were penniless, if they died under Jewish persecution, nor do we know if they were young parents, or was Esther born to them late in life. All we know is that she didn't have a father or mother. Again, the self-perception of being an orphan is different than children growing up with a father and mother to whom they can relate.

Adopted. After Esther's parents died, her cousin Mordecai adopted her and raised her. "He [Mordecai] had brought up Hadassah, that is, Esther, his uncle's daughter . . . took her as his own daughter" (Est. 2:7). Therefore, Esther and Mordecai were doubly related. First, as cousins; and second, in an adoptive role. Probably Esther was not adopted officially as Americans legally adopt today. She was probably just brought into Mordecai's family to be raised as one of his children. However, Esther was called "Queen Esther, the daughter of Abihail, with Mordecai the Jew" (Est. 9:29).

Attractive. What is known about Esther's physical makeup? The Bible says "the young woman was lovely and beautiful" (Est. 2:7). However, her great inner character enhanced her outer beauty. When she won the beauty contest to become Queen of all Persia, it was probably a combination of her total personality, not just her physical attractiveness.

Unobservable influence. God works His influence through people who many times can't outwardly serve or testify to Him. Such was the case of Esther. As a matter of fact, even her Hebrew name Hadassah was predictive of how God would use her. The name *Hadassah* means "myrtle," which was a bush that grows under a canopy of trees. The beauty of myrtle is protected from the sun by other bushes or trees. And then again, her Gentile name, Esther, is also predictive of her future influence. The name *Esther* means "star." When the sun is burning brightly, stars cannot be seen. But during the night and when you "walk through the valley of the shadow of death," you have the stars to guide you. When Israel walked through the death valley of possible annihilation, Esther was the star who guided them to safety.

Because of her unnoticed influence, Esther didn't let people know that she was a Jew. When she entered the "Miss Persia" contest, her adoptive father Mordecai counseled her not to tell anyone about her background. "Esther had not revealed her people or family" (Est. 2:10).

> "For if you remain completely silent at this time, relief and deliverance will arise for the Jews from another place, but you and your father's house will perish. Yet who knows whether you have come to the kingdom for such a time as this?" (Est. 4:14).

Esther's strategy. When the prime minister Haman wanted to destroy all Jews, Esther was used of God to stop this Jewish holocaust. Mordecai would not bow down to worship Haman, and in vengeful anger, Haman tricked King Xerxes to sign a decree that anyone who killed a Jew could keep their money and property. Thus, Haman plotted a divisive plan to get rid of not only Mordecai, but all Jews in the world. What would Esther do? What could she do? Mordecai told her.

The story is well known how Esther fasted for three days, then appeared before the king. Everyone knew that if the king didn't hold out his scepter to Esther when she appeared in his court, she could have been punished, even killed. But her beauty won the day! King Xerxes agreed to attend a banquet at Esther's home. But at that banquet Esther, a woman sure of herself, didn't tell her husband, Xerxes, what she wanted. She made him promise to come back a second night for a second banquet. It was then that the evil plan of Haman was revealed to Xerxes. As a matter of fact, Haman was hanged on the gallows that he had prepared for Mordecai.

"The Jews gathered together in their cities throughout all the provinces of King Ahasuerus to lay hands on those who sought their harm. And no one could withstand them, because fear of them fell upon all people. . . . Thus the Jews defeated all their enemies with the stroke of the sword, with slaughter and destruction, and did what they pleased with those who hated them. The remainder of the Jews in the king's provinces gathered together and protected their lives, had rest from their enemies, and killed seventy-five thousand of their enemies; but they did not lay a hand on the plunder" (Est. 9:2, 5, 16).

But there remained a problem. The laws of the Medes and Persians indicated that once the king signed a law, it couldn't be reversed or cancelled. Therefore, the king could not stop the imminent Jewish holocaust. But Esther used her influence to supercede the decree with a higher law, i.e., that Jews could defend themselves when attacked, and collect the money and property of those who tried to kill them. As a result, on that fateful day, the Jews successfully defended themselves. Therefore, many people believed in Jehovah God of the Jews.

Artaxerxes Was Probably the Son of Esther

Influence through her son. No one knows for sure if Artaxerxes was the son of Esther, because King Xerxes had a number of wives and a number of concubines. However, many Bible scholars believe Artaxerxes was Esther's son because (1) Esther was identified as Queen, and usually the son of the king and identified queen was next in line of succession. (2) Artaxerxes had a "warm spot" in his heart for the cause of Jews in the capital city, Jerusalem. Why? Because the blood of Queen Esther flowed in his veins.

Principles Learned from Esther

God can use adopted children. Sometimes adopted children feel "cut off from the rest of the world because they don't have an identifiable biological parent as most other children. Sometimes it's because they haven't been raised by their biological parents. Those who are adopted should know that God can use them greatly, as He did Queen Esther.

Those who adopt can influence the world through their children. A multitude of adoptive parents have raised a child and they sometimes wonder what will become of their adopted child. Adoptive parents should recognize that their child can be used greatly of God; adoption is never an issue whether God can or will use a child or not. Think of all the benefits that came to Mordecai because he adopted Esther.

Character is more important than family heritage. Esther had royal blood of King Saul running through her veins, but that was not what made her an outstanding queen. Also, she had outward beauty and that was not the criteria that made her a great queen. The most important thing about Esther was her character. Because of her character—not her birth—God was able to use her greatly to save the Jews from extinction.

> "And all the officials of the provinces, the satraps, the governors, and all those doing the king's work, helped the Jews, because the fear of Mordecai fell upon them. For Mordecai was great in the king's palace, and his fame spread throughout all the provinces; for this man Mordecai became increasingly prominent" (Est. 9:3, 4).

You don't have to be a "tinkling bell" to be influential for God. Esther didn't seek power or fame; rather, she kept her Jewish ancestry secret. She didn't seek to use her role as queen to get her way. Rather, she wisely used her wisdom to save God's people.

Influenced by the Grandson, Artaxerxes

The hidden hand of God. Some doubt if Artaxerxes was the son of Esther; others are sure that Esther was his mother. The question ought to be asked, "If Artaxerxes were the son of Esther and Xerxes, why is it not clear in secular history"? Perhaps it is not clear because that's the way God works. He doesn't tell us everything He does, nor does He show everything He is doing. We don't have to know how God is working, or why God is working, to understand and appreciate the hand of God. Robert Dick, a historian, said, concerning whether Artaxerxes is a son of Esther or not, "It probably will remain forever a mystery."[1] Perhaps in Heaven we will know.

Becoming a Christian for the wrong reason. One of the reasons God hides many things is to produce *truth-faith* in those who believe in Him. If everyone knew clearly what God was doing, they would try to become Christians for the wrong reasons. Notice the phrase, "try to become." If the unsaved knew God made some people rich, they'd get saved for money. If they knew God healed, they'd get saved for good health. The problem is, you can't become a Christian for the wrong reasons, for then your salvation would not be based upon faith (see Eph. 2:8, 9). By faith, we accept God for who He is, and what He's done for us on Calvary. By faith, we yield to God even though we don't always understand why God works, nor do we understand all the things that He does. While some call this "blind faith," it is simply trusting God for salvation, and not trusting anything else.

Why did Artaxerxes choose Nehemiah? When King Artaxerxes chose members of his court, he obviously chose a Jewish cupbearer to be near to him. A cupbearer not only served the king his meals, but in a subtle way was the "secret service," i.e., protection for the king. Because people would try to poison the king, the cupbearer would have to taste the wine first to determine its integrity. Artaxerxes could trust a "Jewish brother" because of their same faith. Also, the book of Nehemiah indicates that he was a physically "overpowering" man. He could guard the king from any physical assault.

What was Nehemiah's passion. Even though Nehemiah was the king's cupbearer, and lived in the palace in Shushan, the most beautiful palace at that time, Nehemiah loved another city more deeply. Jerusalem was his passion. News reached Nehemiah that "the wall of Jerusalem is also broken down, and its gates are burned with fire" (Neh. 1:3). Because of his passion, Nehemiah was overcome with grief. "So it was, when I heard these words, that I sat down and wept, and mourned for many days" (Neh 1:4).

How did Artaxerxes learn of Jerusalem's problems? Because of the king's relationship to his Jewish cupbearer, Artaxerxes learned of Jerusalem. Nehemiah confessed, "I had never been sad in his presence before. Therefore the king said to me, 'Why is your face sad . . . ?'" (Neh 2:1, 2). The big thing in Nehemiah's life was *prayer*. Even though Nehemiah was physically large, prayer had a large place in his life. When he wrote his book, he included the actual prayers that he spontaneously prayed in time of need. So, those who read the book of Nehemiah actually pray the same prayer that Nehemiah prayed. So, what did Nehemiah do when the king asked about his sadness? "So I prayed to the God of heaven" (Neh. 2:4). Is prayer not a good thing for you to do when you are sad about things in your life?

A bad time to request help. When Nehemiah asked for help to rebuild Jerusalem, it was not the best of times in the Persian Empire. Whereas King Cyrus and King Darius had been strong dominant kings, King Artaxerxes was having difficulty keeping his empire together. There were revolutions in Egypt, Greece and Cyprus. He had a general who led an insurrection in Syria, and was leading one of Artaxerxes' own aries to attack him. In spite of all these problems, Artaxerxes gave attention to Jerusalem and was determined to do something. The king's attention to Jerusalem might be another reason to prove he had Jewish blood flowing in his veins.

Why was Artaxerxes' action unusual? The Jews had a long history of rebellion against anyone who tried to subjugate or rule over them. The Jews not only fought against their neighbors, they argued among themselves. Because they were so contentious, who would want to help the Jews, except perhaps another Jew? The small nations round Jerusalem opposed the rebuilding of the wall. They didn't want anything to strengthen the hand of the Jews in the area. At that time, the Jews had rebuilt the temple where they worshipped. But because there were no protective walls around the city, there was no centralized fortress to protect them from marauding bands of thieves or invading armies. But the issue was more than protective walls. The walls were symbolic of the nation being reconstituted. The walls meant the Jews would once again be a self-governing people.

When King Artaxerxes' kingdom was in turmoil, he paused the affairs of the kingdom to look after a small item, i.e., the rebuilding of the walls in Jerusalem, another demonstration of how God works behind the scenes to bring about His plan.

How did Artaxerxes help rebuild Jerusalem? Obviously, the king couldn't travel to Jerusalem, nor could he send his army to help build the walls. King Artaxerxes did two things: first, he granted a letter of authority to Nehemiah to complete the task. "I [Nehemiah] said to the king, 'If it pleases the king, let letters be given to me for the governors of the region'" (Neh. 2:7). Second, Nehemiah knew that money and resources were needed to rebuild the walls. "A letter to Asaph the keeper of the king's forest, that he must give me timber to make beams for the gates of the citadel which pertains to the temple, for the city wall, and for the house that I will occupy. And the king granted them to me according to the good hand of my God upon me" (Neh. 2:8).

How influential was Artaxerxes in God's plan? Even though Artaxerxes was not recognized as a Jew, his influence continued to bless the Jewish people throughout his reign. Just as the previous influence of Mordecai and Esther had been unobservable by the Jews, the same unobservable influence continued in the life of King Artaxerxes.

The Jews had self-government. The Jews had first returned from captivity in 536 AD when King Cyrus of Persia granted a decree permitting the Jews to return to Palestine. King Cyrus didn't do this just because he felt kindly to the Jews; rather, he wanted them to go home to work so he could tax their farms and make money for the Persian Empire. As long as the Jews were held in captivity, the empire had to feed, clothe, and pay soldiers to guard them. There was a second return by the Jews in 516 AD where they set up worship under the open skies and eventually built Zerubbabel's

Temple. But the Jews did not have a central seat of authority. They were just a loose confederation of Jewish families, joined together by their common love of the land and common ancestry.

Jerusalem was the rallying point. The Jews in the Promised Land needed to rebuild the city of Jerusalem for protection from the bands of outlaws and invading armies that swept through the Holy Land. Without their capital city, the Jews didn't have self-respect, nor did they have strong self-identification. The rebuilding of the walls represented the reconstitution of the nation.

The prophecy clock started ticking. When King Artaxerxes signed the decree to rebuild the walls of Jerusalem, something happened in Heaven. The Jews everywhere were praying and begging God to reestablish the kingdom, i.e., the Davidic throne. But the kingdom was not God's immediate plan. God had instituted a program known as "the time of the Gentiles," an era when Gentiles would rule over the Jews (Luke 21:24). This "time of the Gentiles" would extend until the Second Coming of David's son, i.e., Jesus Christ, when He returns to earth to set up His Kingdom.

"He [Jesus] will be great, and will be called the Son of the Highest; and the Lord God will give Him the throne of His father David. And He will reign over the house of Jacob forever, and of His kingdom there will be no end" (Luke 1:32).

So, when King Artaxerxes gave the command to re-establish the walls of Jerusalem, the prophetic clock started ticking. Daniel had been told by God, "From the going forth of the command [454 BC] to restore and build Jerusalem, until Messiah the Prince, there shall be seven weeks and sixty-two weeks [a total of 69 weeks or 483 years]; the street shall be built again, and the wall, even in troublesome times. And after . . . Messiah shall be cut off [30 AD, when Jesus died]" (Dan. 9:25, 26).

Students of prophecy are amazed that God would indicate the exact time when Messiah would be cut off, i.e., Jesus would die for the sins of the people. The date of 454 BC—when the nation was reconstituted—is not a major notation to most people reading the Bible but for the serious student, it is a dividing line of history. Like the myrtle, whose flower is not seen because of the canopy of trees, and like the night star that is not seen in the brilliance of the bright sun, the date of the death of the Messiah is predicted in Scripture, but only a few take note. All three—Mordecai, Esther, Artaxerxes—had learned a principle that the great hand of God moves in unobserved obscurity.

How to Be Influential When People Don't Know You Are a Christian

Hidden influence. Just as Grandpa Mordecai and Queen Esther used their hidden influence for God, grandson Artaxerxes followed their example. While Artaxerxes couldn't tell everyone what he was doing, he let his unobserved influence count in the plan of God. Children who are molded by unobserved influence can be used by God in the same way when their grandparents influence them. But remember, the way God uses grandparents in the life of their grandchildren is the way the young will use their influence for God.

When you can't be outwardly Christian. Just as Esther and Artaxerxes couldn't outwardly demonstrate their faith, you may find yourself in a place where you can't be outwardly Christian. What can you do? You can be faithful to God as they were. You can be influential for God in unobserved obscurity.

Great events usually occur in seemingly small ways. God doesn't always have to use an army to destroy Goliath, i.e., the largest giant in the Philistine nation. God can use a seemingly small boy with a sling to accomplish His purpose. Whether God uses five barley loaves and two small fish to feed approximately 5,000 hungry people, or whether God uses Paul's nephew to save him from an ambush, God many times accomplishes His work in seemingly small ways.

Don't despair in the blackest night. The message of Esther is that in the blackest of nights, the stars shine brightest. Esther's name means *star.* She didn't get a chance to be influential for God until the enemy had seemingly won the day, i.e., the holocaust of the entire Jewish nation. But in that black night, God used the shining star of one woman to save an entire nation.

The future unfolds in seemingly small ways. When King Artaxerxes decreed that Jerusalem's wall could be built, most observers didn't get too excited. After all, the Jews fought among themselves and the nations round about them squabbled with them all the time. Also, King Artaxerxes couldn't send his workmen or armies to help complete the walls. But one man—Nehemiah—rallied the people of Jerusalem so that common people rebuilt the entire wall in 52 days.

The miraculous book of non-miracles. As you read the book of Nehemiah, God doesn't perform outward supernatural miracles. No one is healed, the death angel doesn't visit Israel's enemies and God doesn't roll back the waters of the Red Sea. Rather, each man worked diligently on the wall in front of his own home. Sacrificially working day and night, they completed the task in 52 days. What was seemingly an impossible task, and with seemingly insurmountable obstacles, was overcome by human determination, i.e., the work of God, the way He works today.

Note

1. E. W. Bullinger, *The Companion Bible* (Grand Rapids: Kregel Publications), n.p.

10

Jonathan:

Grandson of Moses

Why Grandchildren Fall into False Teaching

GRANDFATHER—MOSES
FATHER—GERSHOM
GRANDSON—JONATHAN

*"Then the children of Dan set up for themselves the carved image;
and Jonathan the son of Gershom, the son of Moses, and his sons were priests
to the tribe of Dan until the day of the captivity of the land."*

JUDGES 18:30

My name is Jonathan. I am the grandson of a famous grandfather in the Levite family. That makes me a priest. Not many people would remember my father Gershom. He was a priest to Joshua. He didn't do miracles . . . he didn't talk face-to-face with God . . . but he was a good man. He was very faithful to God.

Everybody knows my grandfather Moses. When the Jews were in slavery, it was my grandfather Moses who performed ten miraculous plagues on Egypt until Pharaoh let Israel go. It was my grandfather Moses who waved his staff to divide the Red Sea, and all the people walked over on dry land. It was my grandfather who led the people by that staff through the wilderness. And with that staff, my grandfather smote the rock and water came out.

My grandfather Moses received the Ten Commandments from God and established a new nation. When God's people sinned by worshipping the golden calf, it was my grandfather who was the intercessor that wouldn't let God destroy the Jews.

I want to be famous like my grandfather, but I don't want to do it his way. I want to do my own thing. I want everyone to look up to me when I walk into the campfire. I want to be the big man.

So let me tell you what I'm doing now. I met this man named Micah who asked me to be the priest for his family. I built a shrine and offered sacrifices for his family. The priest from the Tabernacle tells me I'm wrong. They tell me I must sacrifice on the brazen altar at the Tabernacle. They tell me the presence of God is in the Shekinah glory cloud above the Tabernacle. The priests in the Tabernacle call me rebellious, but I think I'm right in my heart. Shouldn't I worship God the way I want to worship Him? Why should I go to Shiloh? Why should I worship God at the brazen altar in the Tabernacle?

When the tribe of Dan broke away from Israel, they needed a priest. It was a chance to become a big leader like my grandfather Moses. So, I left the house of Micah and became a priest of the tribe of Dan. The tribe of Dan stole an idol and set it up for worship. I know my grandfather wouldn't worship idols, but the people can worship better when they can see a carved replica in front of them when they pray.

The priests from the Tabernacle tell me I'm wrong. I tell them I'm doing what my grandfather did. They say if I'm like my grandfather Moses, where are my miracles? They say if I'm like my grandfather Moses, why don't I talk face-to-face with God? They say if I'm like my grandfather Moses, why don't I keep the commandments given by my grandfather.

I may not have the Shekinah-glory cloud, but the people love me . . . they follow me . . . and pay me a good salary. What else do I need?

Moses the Famous Grandfather

Lessons to Take Away

When grandchildren become doctrinal prodigals, their grandparents can take definite steps to influence them to return to the Word of God.

Moses was a brilliant leader. We say that because the Scriptures say, "Moses was learned in all the wisdom of the Egyptians, and was mighty in words and deeds" (Acts 7:22). This is the man who stuttered at the beginning of his ministry, and didn't want to face Pharaoh because of weak speech. But God used the early education he received in Pharaoh's palace to later develop great leadership ability.

Moses was humble. But all of Moses' ability and accomplishments didn't go to his head. God said of him, "Now the man Moses was very humble, more than all men who were on the face of the earth" (Num. 12:3).

Moses set up a worship system and sanctuary for God's people. Beside all of his great accomplishments, perhaps the greatest was leading the nation to worship the Lord. "Now it came to pass, when Moses had finished setting up the tabernacle, that he anointed it and consecrated it and all its furnishings, and the altar and all its utensils; so he anointed them and consecrated them" (Num. 7:1).

Sometimes children have difficulty walking in the footsteps of famous fathers. Maybe it's because children see the greatness of their fathers, and are intimidated by the fact that they think they cannot compare with their father. So, what could the children of Moses expect to accomplish?

Sometimes circumstances make great leaders, and when the crisis goes away, their children never achieve greatness, because they do not face a great challenge as did their father. So the children of Moses would never become as great as their father because they didn't face Egypt, nor did they have to cross the desert.

Gershom: A Famous Father and an Infamous Son

Nothing much is said in the Scriptures about Gershom, son of Moses. He wasn't known for miracles, he didn't preach great sermons, he didn't win great battles, nor did he begin a new movement for God. When Gershom was young, he was probably introduced to the crowd as the son of a great father. Later in Gershom's life he would be introduced as the father of an infamous son who disobeyed Jehovah. Gershom was the father of Jonathan, a false teacher and an apostate.

The name Gershom meant *stranger*. When Gershom was first born, Moses gave him the name that reflected his location in the desert. Moses had been run out of Egypt because he was wanted for murder. He became a shepherd in the backside of the desert. Moses couldn't return home to his adoptive parents in Pharaoh's palace, nor could he return to his Jewish people who were slaves. When Gershom was born to him in the desert, he named his son "stranger." "And she [Zipporah] bore him a son. He called his name Gershom, for he said, I have been a stranger in a foreign land" (Ex. 2:22).

Jonathan: A Grandson's Fall from Greatness

Moses, the greatest Hebrew leader of all times, had a grandson who denied the principle for which Moses stood. However, it didn't start out that way. When grandson Jonathan was born, he was given the name "Jehovah has given." Jonathan's name should have provided spiritual direction for his life. But Jonathan's life denied the meaning of his name.

> The sons of famous men
> are not usually famous themselves.

Moses was born in the family tribe of Levi, which meant he was from the *priest-tribe* for the nation of Israel. Moses could sacrifice to God for the people. That meant Gershom could do the same thing, i.e., Gershom was a priest of God. It also meant Jonathan was a priest.

Jonathan wanted to be a famous leader like his grandfather Moses, but he tried to do it apart from Moses' integrity. Jonathan went to ministry as a priest for Micah and his family. By Jonathan's own confession he said, "Micah . . . has hired me, and I have become his priest" (Judg. 18:4). Previously Micah had stolen some money from his mother, but later restored it to her. Since she had already dedicated the money for an idol, she took two hundred shekels (five pounds) and had an idol sculptured out of the money. Micah set up a private shrine—in his home—and ordained one of his sons to be his priest. But that didn't satisfy Micah because his son was not from the tribe of Levi. When Jonathan was traveling through the area, Micah convinced Jonathan to become his priest, agreeing to pay him an annual salary, plus provide food and clothing.

During this time, the tribe of Dan was migrating from the territory assigned to it in the South; they were traveling to the north. Five spies from the Danites noticed the shrine at Micah's house, along with its monetary value. When they left, Jonathan wished them, "God bless you" on their evil journey. Later the Danites returned to pillage Micah's shrine, steal his idols, and force Jonathan to go with him as their priest. They attacked Laish, a quiet and secure valley, killed all of the people, and burned the city with fire. Then the Danites settled down in the valley with Jonathan as their priest. Symbolically, Jonathan set up a *worship war* in opposition to the Tabernacle of God that was at Shiloh, where the Shekinah glory cloud and presence of God rested on the Ark of the Covenant.

Grandfather Moses spoke to God face-to-face, and received the Ten Commandments from the hand of God; yet Grandson Jonathan denied all that was taught in the five books of the Law written by Moses. The grandson became a false teacher and an apostate.

Jonathan tried to serve the Lord like his grandfather Moses, but was not called of God. Moses was called of God at the burning bush, but Jonathan didn't evidence a supernatural call of God upon his life. As a matter of fact, Jonathan was "called" by a man, Micah. "Micah consecrated the Levite [Jonathan], and the young man became his priest" (Judg. 17:12).

Those who are willing to serve the Lord for money naturally go to another place for service when a better offer comes along.

Notice Jonathan's response: "His heart was glad."
(Judges 18:20)

Jonathan later yielded to pressure. After serving Micah as priest, an army of six hundred Danites came to Micah's house and stood before the Shrine, intimidating Jonathan. "Six hundred warriors from the tribe of Dan stood just outside the gate . . . be quiet and come with us, they said" (Judg. 18:16, 19, *NLB*). If Jonathan were a man of God, he could not be intimidated by soldiers. Surely his grandfather Moses was never intimidated by Pharaoh or his armies.

Jonathan wanted the vast influence of his grandfather Moses, but didn't yield to the influence of God. Moses led the entire nation of Israel; where does that leave Grandson Jonathan? Obviously the nation didn't turn to Jonathan for leadership. When God's people look for a leader, they always choose one with character and Jonathan wasn't a man of spiritual character.

Jonathan was a "climber." First, he became a priest for one family, then he became a priest for one tribe. The men of Dan said to him, "Isn't it better to be a priest for an entire tribe of Israel than just for the household of one man?" (Judg. 18:19). So Jonathan settled to be priest over the smallest of the twelve tribes. Obviously he would never be God's man for the entire nation.

> Character is habitually doing the right
> thing in the right way.

Jonathan wanted the supernatural power of his grandfather Moses, but was treated by the people as a "good luck charm." People did not look up to Jonathan as a man of God. When Micah finally hired Jonathan to be his priest, what is Micah's response? "Now I know the Lord will bless me seeing I have hired a Levite as my priest" (Judg. 17:13, author's translation). Jonathan became a good luck charm to Micah's household. Just like people rub a rabbit's foot to get what they want, or people keep good luck charms for protection from evil, that's how the family of Micah treated Jonathan.

Jonathan's Sin

Incomplete Obedience. Jonathan should have been an obedient priest who worshipped God correctly. The Tabernacle was at Shiloh, the place where sacrifices were brought to God for the forgiveness of sin. As people approached the Tabernacle at Shiloh, they could see a smoke cloud lofting into Heaven, i.e., the Shekinah-glory cloud that indicated the presence of God. Jonathan should have taken his place at Shiloh along with the other priests before the Lord at the door of the Tabernacle (see Josh. 19:31).

When a beginning minister gets away from the
local church, he's heading for trouble.

There's nothing magical about a local church that keeps a minister from drifting away from God. However, there is *accountability* in a local church; because people are watching him. As they worship together, the priest becomes accountable to the people he leads. But also, the church produces *responsibility.* When a priest is responsible for the spiritual welfare of people, it keeps him responsible in prayer and holiness. When today's minister thinks he is too big for the church, or thinks he doesn't need the church, or tries to live without the church, he is heading for trouble.

Obvious disobedience. When Jonathan first showed up at Micah's house, he saw the idol that Micah had made from the collected money donated by his mother, i.e., a five-pound idol. Jonathan should have known the law of God, after all, his grandfather Moses received the Ten Commandments on Mt. Sinai. Jonathan had probably memorized the Ten Commandments and repeated them as a young boy in his father's tent. He should have known the Second Commandment, "You shall not make for yourself a carved image . . . you shall not bow down to them nor serve them.

For I, the LORD your God, am a jealous God, visiting the iniquity of the fathers upon the children to the third and fourth generations" (Ex. 20:4, 5).

Because of Jonathan's disobedience, it is no wonder that he became a reprobate priest for the Danites for his whole life, and so did his children after him, "until the day of the captivity" (Judg. 18:30).

Jonathan sold out for money. We find that when Jonathan first met Micah, Micah said, "I will give you ten shekels of silver" (Judg. 17:10). Doesn't false teaching usually begin in the lust of the flesh, the lust of the eyes or the pride of life?

Jonathan sold out for security. Micah not only promised him money, but also said, "I will give you . . . a suit of clothes" (Judg. 17:10).

Flagrant heresy. Rather than going to the house of God at Shiloh, Jonathan set up his own separate shrine for the Danites in Laish. How long did he keep this separate house of worship? "All the time that the house of God was in Shiloh" (Judg. 18:31).

Why Was This Heresy?

1. Jonathan didn't worship God in the Tabernacle.
2. He substituted his own worship.
3. He deceived the people because God was not in it.
4. His actions kept the Danites from worshipping God in the Tabernacle.

Arrogantly deceptive. Jonathan falsely claimed to speak for God. On one occasion he told the Danites, "Go in peace. The presence of the LORD be with you on your way" (Judg. 18:6). He knew where the Danites were going, i.e., away from the land allotted to them by God. He should have known about rebellion, and he should have known that they were going to illegally occupy someone else's territory. But Jonathan wishes them, "Godspeed." What happened to the Danites that Jonathan blessed? They slaughtered the people of Laish, stole their property, burned their city and occupied their land.

Perplexing question. As we look at the spiraling fall of Jonathan from the lofty beginning of his life into false teaching and apostasy, we must ask ourselves the question, "Why?" Since we can't look at his heart, we can only see the outward motives that influenced the direction of his life. These outward motives seem to be money, pleasing men, and perhaps the unseen motive of pride. Jonathan had forgotten what his grandfather had taught, i.e., "You shall love the LORD your God with all your heart, with all your soul, and with all your strength" (Deut. 6:5).

Helping a Doctrinal Prodigal

Pray for the prodigal. Two grandparents should covenant together to pray for grandchildren who are slipping into false teaching. The agreement of two grandparents lifts their prayer to a higher level and can bring a more definite answer. Why? Because Jesus promised, "Again I say to you that if two of you agree on earth concerning anything that they ask, it will be done for them by My Father in heaven" (Matt. 18:19).

Become intentional in their life. When your grandchildren begin to slip into error, don't turn your back on them, nor ignore their problem. You must give diligence to do something about the problem and solve it if you can. First, you must not ignore what is happening in the life of a grandchild, second determine to do something about it, and third, take action. "Brethren, if anyone among you wanders from the truth, and someone turns him back, let him know that he who turns a sinner from the error of his way will save a soul from death and cover a multitude of sins" (Jas. 5:19, 20).

Point out differences between where they're going and where they've been. This does not mean you should argue or debate with your straying grandchild. Sometimes you can win an argument, but you lose the grandchild. But you should make sure that your grandchild understands there is a difference between light and darkness, between truth and error. "We are of God. He who knows God hears us; he who is not of God does not hear us. By this we know the spirit of truth and the spirit of error" (1 John 4:6).

Quietly explain the truth. The Bible says that "A soft answer turns away wrath" (Prov. 15:1). So when you talk with your grandchildren, speak softly, but make sure your answer is based on the Word of God. Remember, "Aquila and Priscilla . . . took him [Apollos] aside and explained to him the way of God more accurately" (Acts 18:26).

Your grandchild's reasons for going into false teaching are not usually their root reason. Usually there are subversive reasons why grandchildren drift from the faith or deny the faith. Sometimes it's bitterness over a legalistic home. And other times it's because of hidden sin in their life, or they've given into the lust of eyes, the lust of the flesh, or the pride of life (see 1 John 2:15, 16). When grandchildren try to deny God or the Bible, and give you academic reasons for their apostasy, there is usually a deeper reason why they have turned from the faith. Notice Paul told Timothy people strayed from the faith because of money: "For the love of money is a root of all kinds of evil, for which some have strayed from the faith in their greediness" (1 Tim. 6:10).

Always love them. No matter how eloquent your grandchildren, and no matter how vile their sin; always love them. No matter how well they argue, and no matter how sound their reasons for leaving Christianity, always love them. When you can't reach them any other way, you can reach across the miles with love and prayer. Notice, "But when he [the Prodigal Son] was still a great way off, his father saw him and had compassion, and ran and fell on his neck and kissed him" (Luke 15:20).

11

Noah:

Grandfather of Canaan

When Grandparents Become a Stumbling Block to Grandchildren

GRANDFATHER—NOAH—*SINNED*
FATHER—HAM—*GOSSIPED*
GRANDSON—CANAAN—*LAUGHED*

"And Noah began to be a farmer, and he planted a vineyard. Then he drank of the wine and was drunk, and became uncovered in his tent. And Ham, the father of Canaan, saw the nakedness of his father, and told his two brothers outside. But Shem and Japheth took a garment, laid it on both their shoulders, and went backward and covered the nakedness of their father. Their faces were turned away, and they did not see their father's nakedness. So Noah awoke from his wine, and knew what his younger son had done to him. Then he said: Cursed be Canaan; a servant of servants he shall be to his brethren."

Genesis 9:20-25

My name is Noah and you all know me because I built the ark. And you know about the flood that covered the entire earth. But today I am not here to talk about the flood. I want to talk to you about my grandson Canaan. This is a difficult story to tell because all grandfathers have difficulty when their grandsons turn evil.

But there is another aspect of the story that embarrasses me. I got drunk and sinned and my sin hurt my grandson. Of all the people who should have known about drunkenness, it was me. Remember, for years I warned everyone that God was going to judge the world with a flood. No one would listen to me because people were giving themselves over to drunkenness, and sexual perversion. They were dabbling in demonism and worshiping Satan. I should have known what would happen to me when I got drunk because I saw what God did to the world; He judged them.

Before the flood, I was a carpenter, and a pretty good one at that. I built something that no one else had ever built in history. I built the biggest thing a man had ever built, 450 feet long, 3 stories tall, and 75 feet wide. I built a boat, just me and my three sons. In your day, that's as big as a large 3-story apartment building. And let me tell you how good my boat was: it didn't break up in 40 days of storms. It floated for an entire year, saving me and my wife, and three sons and their wives.

After the flood I gave up carpentry and went into farming. I grew all my food, and I especially enjoyed some sweet luscious grapes. Mm-m-m-m-m! They were mouth-watering good every time I put a grape in my mouth. One day after making sweet crushed grape juice, I absentmindedly left a bucket of grape juice hanging on a peg in the storehouse. I didn't know what fermentation was, but the sweet grapes rotted and then fermented. Just as I was going to throw that bucket out, I smelled a different fragrance and decided to taste it. You know, it only takes one taste for a man to become an alcoholic. One drink led to another and before I knew what happened, I was drunk.

I only tasted a little at first, then got so drunk I passed out. That's when the terrible act occurred. I was drunk on the floor, naked and had passed out. My grandson Canaan came in and that's when the sin happened. God hates sin; it's so bad I can't describe it in public.

But my son Ham—that's Canaan's father—was horrified, but he didn't do anything. He could have covered me, but he didn't. The only thing he did was run to tell his brothers. My other two sons, Japheth and Shem, walked in backwards with a sheet over their shoulders to cover me. I'm thankful for that.

Sometimes a man curses because he is mad; sometimes a man will even curse in God's name. But the cursing that took place that day was different. It wasn't just me cursing my grandson; it was God speaking through me. For God saw in Canaan a sexual weakness and lustful appetite. God knew that his sin would be perpetrated upon his children and passed on to their children, and they in turn would have the same influence on their children. So, I spoke God's curse upon Canaan,

"Cursed [be] Canaan; A servant of servants He shall be to his brethren" (Gen. 9:25).

I don't know what's going to happen to that boy, nor do I know what will happen to his succeeding generations. But I do know grandparents must be careful to live a godly life before their grandchildren. I also know the sin of grandparents can have disastrous consequences on their grandchildren.

What Happened That Day?

Lessons to Take Away
Sin in the life of a grandparent can have a disastrous influence on grandchildren.

Wine is first mentioned in the Bible when Noah became a farmer, planted grapes, and eventually got drunk off of the fruit of his harvest. When Noah preached against sin before the flood, he probably included the sin of "drinking" (Matt. 24:38). Though Noah was guilty of the sin of drunkenness, carelessness, and being a negative role model, the sin of Canaan was much more serious. Canaan's sin revealed perhaps his suppressed carnal attitude towards sin, or his rebellious attitude towards his grandfather, and perhaps a resentment against God in Heaven.

When Noah awoke from his drunkenness, he spoke the words of a curse over his grandson Canaan, which were probably the words of God who knew the sins of Canaan's heart. God, who alone knows the future, looked down the hallway of time and knew that the grandson Canaan's sin towards Noah's nakedness would be carried out in the sexual sins of the Canaanite nations that lived in the Promised Land. When Joshua destroyed the Canaanites and drove them from the Promise Land, he carried out the curse of Noah against Canaan.

What We Know for Sure

Noah was godly. When the entire face of the earth was given over to sin, God could only find one righteous family, and through that family, God determined to save mankind. "Noah found grace in the eyes of the Lord . . . Noah was a just man and perfect in his generation, and Noah walked with God" (Gen. 6:8, 9).

Noah warned the world of coming judgment. God revealed to Noah that He was going to destroy the earth. "And the LORD said, My Spirit shall not strive with man forever, for he is indeed flesh" (Gen. 6:3). Why would God destroy them? "Then the Lord saw that the wickedness of man was great in the earth, and that every intent of the thoughts of his heart was only evil continually. And the Lord was sorry that He had made man on the earth, and He was grieved in His heart. So the Lord said, I will destroy man whom I have created from the face of the earth, both man and beast, creeping thing and birds of the air, for I am sorry that I have made them" (Gen. 6:5-7).

God spoke to Noah—whether audibly or internally—warning him of the coming flood. "By faith Noah, being divinely warned of things not yet seen, moved with godly fear, prepared an ark . . . by which he condemned the world" (Heb. 11:7).

Originally Noah was a carpenter. His occupation before the flood was building things, probably the houses for the godly line of Seth. And then God said, "Make yourself an ark of gopherwood" (Gen. 6:14). This was no ordinary boat (the word ark means box). The ark was a large floating box (barge) 450 feet long, 75 feet wide, and 50 feet tall (three stories). Noah wasn't just a carpenter; he built massive things (the ark was as large as a large three-story tall college dormitory that is longer than a football field). But Noah was an outstanding carpenter, for the ark he built was able to withstand the storms and torrential rainfall for forty days, and deliver the family safe for the one year they lived in the ark.

Noah was a preacher. The size of the ark was warning in itself to the world that a flood was coming. But more than a vessel of safety, this ark warned the unrighteous people of coming judgment. Noah also preached, "Noah . . . a preacher of righteousness" (2 Pet. 2:5) and warned the people of coming judgment.

The sin of drunkenness. Probably drunkenness was not the primary sin of the generations before the flood. They were guilty of idolatry, sexual perversion, and other sins outlined in Romans 1:1-27 (this would have involved spirit worship, which was probably demon worship). Isn't most idol worship a recognition of the spirit behind the idol, which is usually a demon spirit?

Jesus likened the events prior to the flood to the events prior to His Second Coming to the earth. Jesus said, "But as the days of Noah were, so also will the coming of the Son of Man . . . drinking . . . until the day that Noah entered the ark" (Matt. 24:37, 38). The emphasis here is on drunkenness, because that is the sin of which Noah was guilty in his later life.

When judgment was ready. One week before God opened the heavens to bring forth rain on the earth, God called Noah and his family into the ark. The Lord said, "Come into the ark, you and all your household" (see Gen. 7:1). At the time Noah was six hundred years old (Gen. 8:13). He had not had sons before he was five hundred years old, so his three sons were all under a hundred years old. However, don't compare a hundred-year-old man to our age today. In Noah's age, the body had probably not deteriorated from the accumulated germs and bacteria that infected humans after the Fall in the Garden of Eden. When God warned Adam, "Thou shalt surely die," the Hebrew language says literally, "And dying, thou shalt die." This means that death would be a gradual process, followed by a climactic event. Therefore, the gradual process of deterioration from bacteria did not yet reach its accumulative end in seventy years, that we experience today (Ps. 90:10).

After coming out of the ark, Noah and his family faced a clean new world. There was no sin in the world that they entered into, yet the seed of sin is born in the heart of every child; so the root of sin entered the new world as the children and grandchildren of Noah populated the face of the earth.

> Alcohol is an addictive poison that will make slaves
> of some with only one taste, and after a lifetime
> of drunkenness will destroy your body and mind,
> loosen your self-discipline, turn friends and family
> against you, and destroy your character.

Noah's new occupation. After the flood, Noah changed his occupation from carpentry to farming. "Noah began to be a farmer, and he planted a vineyard" (Gen. 9:20). We cannot imagine that this godly man would purposely have fermented wine, and literally drank to destroy his example before his family, and became drunk to the spiritual destruction of a grandson named Canaan. Most believe that Noah stumbled on the process of fermentation, and once he tasted the "brew," it became addictive.

Noah's threefold sin. The sin was not in simply tasting the wine, but in the entire process that followed. "He [Noah] drank of the wine and was drunk, and became uncovered in his tent" (Gen. 9:21).

Noah's Sin

- Drunkenness—the sin he preached against
- Exposure—he uncovered himself, i.e., *Gulah* (Reflective)
- Destroyed his godly example

How did Noah know? After Noah awoke from his drunkenness, for some reason he knew what had happened. This is an interesting question that deserves some speculation.

- Revelation: God told Noah what happened
- Inquiry: He asked or was told what happened
- Memory: A drunk man remembers some things

What Was the Sin of Ham and Canaan?

Apparently Canaan was the one who discovered his grandfather's nakedness, and did something—we don't know what—that reflected his evil heart. Some say he laughed at Noah, and his relationship to God. Some say it was a sexual act, i.e., a homosexual act. Some say it was something we don't know. In any occasion, Canaan told his father Ham what he saw. When Ham heard about it, he should have done something, i.e., he should have done what his older brothers did. Ham should have put a coat upon his shoulders and backing into the room covered his father's nakedness. But Ham didn't.

Ham told his older brothers about his father's nakedness. It was then that the two older brothers put a covering over their shoulders and backed into the room to cover their father's nakedness. When Noah awoke, he knew what had happened. It was then that God spoke a curse through Noah on Canaan, and his posterity.

Seeing only. The Bible doesn't say that Canaan saw the nakedness of his grandfather, but he was cursed, implying Canaan had done something worse than just looking at his grandfather. Ham just looked: "Ham, the father of Canaan, saw the nakedness of his father, and told his two brothers outside" (Gen. 9:22). What goes with the act of seeing? If Canaan just saw his grandfather's nakedness, why was he cursed, but his father Ham not cursed? The act of looking by Ham could be wrong. Why could the act of observing nudity be wrong?

- Lust
- Mockery
- Rejection of grandfather's spiritual authority
- Didn't cover his nakedness

From all that we can read throughout Scripture, just observing nakedness is not a sin serious enough to be condemned for the next generations. Apparently Canaan did something deeper or more serious. Whatever the deeper sin, it was serious enough to bring God's curse upon Canaan and all those in his biological line.

The two older sons—Shem and Japheth—did not go in to look at their father. This was more than not being curious; they were being respectful. What did they do? "Shem and Japheth took a garment, laid it on both their shoulders, and went backward and covered the nakedness of their father. Their faces were turned away, and they did not see their father's nakedness" (Gen. 9:23).

When Canaan was cursed, Shem and Japheth were blessed. "Blessed be the Lord, the God of Shem" (Gen. 9:26). How was Shem blessed? "May God enlarge Japheth, and may he dwell in the tents of Shem; and may Canaan be his servant" (Gen. 9:27).

As a result of Shem's blessing, he was identified with the worship of Jehovah, and has been recognized as a group of people with dominant spiritual motives. Ultimately, the woman's seed, i.e., the Messiah, came from the family of Shem, through Abraham, and the Jews. Jesus ultimately came from the line of Shem.

God also promised to bless Japheth. The Japhetic peoples are Greeks, Romans, Arians, Europeans, and they have been those who have supplied scientific discovery, philosophers, and been the driving force behind Western civilization.

Why curse Canaan? Ham was the youngest son of Noah, and Canaan was the youngest son of Ham (see Gen. 10:6). Just as people say that the youngest child of the family is the spoiled one, so Ham and Canaan were the youngest in the family; perhaps they received the least amount of attention, discipline, and direction.

A divine curse. When Noah cursed Canaan, this was not just an "angry" grandfather who was punishing his grandson. No! Only God knows the future, so only God knew what the Canaanites would be like long after Noah and his sons were dead. So God cursed Canaan through Noah, because of what would happen to Canaan and his sons, i.e., the Canaanites. God spoke a curse through Noah on Canaan for what he did to his grandfather Noah, predicting that his descendants would do the same thing in the future, hence would be judged by God.

God revealed a weakness in both Ham and Canaan because their sexual weakness would be perpetuated in the Canaanites who occupied the Promised Land. When Noah said, "Cursed be Canaan; A servant of servants He shall be to his brethren" (Gen. 9:25), God was applying the principle that He said elsewhere, i.e., that the third and fourth generation would be punished for the sins of their forefathers, because they too will continue in that sin. "For I, the LORD your God, am a jealous God, visiting the iniquity of the fathers upon the children to the third and fourth generations of those who hate Me" (Exod. 20:5). Did you see that phrase "hate Me"? Implied in the sin of Canaan is a rejection of God, perhaps even hatred of God. This young boy who lived one generation from the flood, was not grateful for the Lord's deliverance through the flood. Rather than showing respect for a grandfather who was used of God, young Canaan thumbed his nose at both Noah, and the God of Noah.

When was Canaan's curse carried out? Some Christians, primarily those from the segregated part of the United States, teach that the curse is on the black man who originally came from Africa and happened when some became slaves to the white man. This obviously is an attempt to justify slavery and segregation. But that view is wrong for more than one reason. First, because the curse was on Canaan, not on Ham. It was Ham who went to Africa; Canaan went to the land named after him, i.e., Canaan. Second, the curse was on Canaan and the Canaanites who lived in the Promised Land. That curse was carried out when God's people—Hebrews, not whites— were led by Joshua to conquer the Promised Land and drive out the Canaanites.

Throughout the early books of Scripture, the Canaanites are described as a lustful people. At one place God described them with an unusual phrase: "uncovered their nakedness" (Lev. 18:3ff), perhaps a description that has its roots in the original reason why God used Israel to drive the Canaanites from Canaan.

What Grandparents Should Know About Sin

You never get too old to sin. Some people think that the older they get, the godlier they become. They don't usually see older people involved in sexual sins, stealing, or the other outward physical sins.

So, they equate the sedate nature of the older people with godliness. But, just being quiet and meek does not make a person godly. To be godly, one must get close to God. To be spiritual, one must be filled with the Holy Spirit (see Eph. 5:18).

Remember, as a young man Solomon served the Lord and wrote the beautiful Song of Solomon. It was the middle-aged Solomon who pursued women, and the bitter old Solomon who wrote the book of Ecclesiastes where he said, "Vanity of vanities, all is vanity" (Eccl. 1:2).

You can fall at your greatest strength. Often in the Bible when God's people fell into sin, they didn't usually fall at their weakness; rather they usually fell at their strength. Abraham was a man of great faith, but in weakness he lied about his wife. God called Moses the meekest man on the face of the earth, yet in pride he smote the rock. Elijah was a bold prophet, yet one word from Jezebel set him running away. Solomon was the wisest man on the face of the earth, yet he "chased skirts." And Peter was the bold disciple, but he denied the Lord with a curse when a little maid challenged him. That means older people can fall at their strength, not weakness. Paul warns us, "Therefore let him who thinks he stands take heed lest he fall" (1 Cor. 10:12).

Your fall can hurt your family. You never sin alone; your sin is like a rock thrown into a pond, creating endless ripples that ultimately will reach the shore. Every sin you commit will have an influence on your children, and grandchildren. Noah's sins certainly condemned his grandson Canaan.

Your sin can come after God has greatly used you. Some of God's greatest leaders had a relapse after they were used greatly of God. On Mount Carmel, Elijah confronted the prophets of Baal, prayed fire out of Heaven and later prayed rain out of Heaven (it had not rained for three and half years) (see Jas. 5:17-18). Yet Elijah ran away from Jezebel, became depressed, and questioned God. Peter was the leader of the twelve disciples but denied the Lord. David drove the enemies out of the Promised Land, and became king over all twelve tribes of Israel; but after great victories, committed adultery with Bathsheba, and was responsible for the murder of Uriah. We read godly King Azziah fortified Israel, yet at the end of his reign became arrogant. He went into the house of God, invaded the office of the priest and tried to sacrifice to God. God immediately struck him with leprosy, and he had to abdicate his throne. It is possible to be greatly used of God, then lose your effectiveness in your last days.

Just because you've done much for God in the past doesn't mean He will overlook sin in your old age. There is no such thing as supererogation whereby you can build up good works in Heaven to compensate for future sins. Every sin stands for itself, just like every good work will have its own reward. A truthful God cannot overlook your sin, just like He will not deny reward for what you do good.

A careless root of sin in a grandfather can have disastrous results in grandchildren. Sometimes older people become careless in their walk for God. Maybe they've sinned several times, and each time God has forgiven and restored them. This can produce a cavalier approach to iniquity. Therefore aged people who know much think they know enough to get away with sin. But it's not true; look again at the case of Noah's disastrous results on Canaan.

Drunkenness is not a private sin, nor is it something God overlooks. Some people think that they harm only themselves when they get drunk. A drunk doesn't say, "Leave me alone," claiming "I'm not hurting anyone." But that's not true. A drunk doesn't have a positive influence on others. A drunk is not a role model of God's grace. A drunk is not influencing children and grandchildren into righteousness. A drunk is not "filled with the spirit" but they are "filled with wine." Paul has told us, "And do not be drunk with wine, in which is dissipation; but be filled with the Spirit" (Eph. 5:18).

The child of God must be modest because the body is the Temple of the Holy Spirit. Obviously most everyone has looked at naked little babies, because most everyone has changed diapers. Why is that we begin to think that nakedness is nothing? Is that why after we get older we take a cavalier approach to nakedness?

Honestly, the body is a beautiful thing, and in certain works of art, people admire the beauty and artistic form of a human body. But nakedness . . . and lust . . . and evil desires are tied to the wrong display of the body, and the wrong viewing of nakedness. Modesty of the body has always been a Christian virtue. The body is the temple of the Holy Spirit (see 1 Cor. 6:18-20). It is a sanctuary because God lives in us; therefore, we must be careful to always glorify God with the body.

- Applies to all ages
- Applies to sexual exposure
- Applies to sexual viewing, i.e., lust

Repressed lust and sexual fantasies usually surface when given the opportunity. Apparently Canaan had some internally negative attitudes towards Noah and the Lord God. When given the opportunity to mock God's man—Noah—Canaan was quick to seize the opportunity. What Canaan said to his father Ham reflected the attitude of his heart.

Sometimes children can be raised in a Christian home, and repress their sexual or rebellious attitudes. But when given an opportunity, "what's in the well comes up in the bucket." When people don't discipline themselves, sin usually finds a way to express itself in looks, attitudes, and actions.

What Grandchildren Need to Know

God provides victory. There is an internal battle between good and evil, and God has provided that every child can overcome temptation. When you daily pray the Lord's Prayer, you ask, "Lead us not into temptation" (Matt. 6:10). As you make that request, claim victory because "no temptation has overtaken you except such as is common to man; but God is faithful, who will not allow you to be tempted beyond what you are able, but with the temptation will also make the way of escape, that you may be able to bear it" (1 Cor. 10:13).

God lives in your body. In this dispensation, God is not living in a tabernacle in the wilderness, nor does He live in a sanctuary like Solomon's Temple in Jerusalem. Rather, God seeks a sanctuary, i.e., the sanctuary of your body. As Paul said, As Paul said, "Christ lives in me" (Gal. 2:20). But that's not just living in your mind; Christ actually lives in your body. Notice what Paul says: "Flee sexual immorality. Every sin that a man does is outside the body, but he who commits sexual immorality sins against his own body. Or do you not know that your body is the temple of the Holy Spirit who is in you, whom you have from God, and you are not your own?" (1 Cor. 6:18-19).

What did Noah do? He filled his body with alcohol, rather than filling his life with God. What was Ham's reaction? Surely he didn't take a godly approach to the sin of his grandfather. And what was Canaan's reaction? He went farther than any other reaction; his sin was greatest of all. If Ham and Canaan had sought the glory of God and the restoration of his grandfather, the curse of Canaan would have never happened.

The old age sin will disqualify you. What is old age sin? It's running the race well, but giving up when you're almost to the finish line. It's living for God all of your life, but denying God when you reach retirement. It's treating your golden years as an opportunity to give up Sunday school teaching, church attendance, and the opportunity to influence your grandchildren.

Paul challenged us to run a race. "Do you not know that those who run in a race all run, but one receives the prize? Run in such a way that you may obtain it" (1 Cor. 9:24). What was that prize that you would obtain? Paul says that we must discipline ourselves as a runner, so we can make it to the finish line. "But I discipline my body and bring it into subjection, lest, when I have preached to others, I myself should become disqualified" (1 Cor. 9:27).

12

Paul:

A Spiritual Grandparent to Timothy's Converts

A Disciple-Making Grandparent

SPIRITUAL GRANDFATHER—PAUL
SON IN MINISTRY—TIMOTHY
THIRD GENERATION—FAITHFUL MEN
FOURTH GENERATION—OTHERS

"And the things that you have heard from me among many witnesses, commit these to faithful men who will be able to teach others also."

2 TIMOTHY 2:2

My name is Timothy. I was born and grew up in a little out-of-the-way mountain village called Lystra. My father was a Gentile who did not follow the God of the Old Testament, but he allowed my grandmother Lois and my mother Eunice—both godly Jewish women—to teach me the Word of God and made sure that I obeyed the God of the Old Testament. Like all good Jewish boys, I was looking for the Messiah. When the apostle Paul came to Lystra, preaching the Lord Jesus Christ, I believed Jesus was the Messiah, and Jesus became my Savior. I remember the first time Paul took me aside, encouraging me to serve the Lord. He took time to answer all my questions. Over the years Paul became my substitute father, and my role model; I decided to be like Paul when I became a man.

When Paul came through our village on his second missionary journey, he asked me to travel with the team. At first, I took care of the luggage, and the tickets, and the meals, and the lodging. Paul was run out of Thessalonica by a mob of hateful Jews; he left me there to preach. I had seen Paul stoned by another mob and I knew it could happen to me, but I was willing to die for the Lord.

On two or three other occasions, Paul sent me to preach and build up the young churches. Finally I became pastor of Ephesus, that great church where Paul had preached. Paul not only taught me the Word of God but he gave me responsibilities to serve the Lord, so I'd grow stronger in character for the Lord Jesus Christ.

My life won't be complete until I influence another young man, like Paul influenced me. I'll have to teach another young man doctrine and give him other responsibilities so he can grow in spiritual character, just as I've grown. And then, that young disciple that I train will have to influence still another young disciple. What Paul poured into me, will have to be poured into other young leaders until the Great Commission is completed, and the world is won to Jesus Christ.

What GRANDPARENTS Do that Parents Don't Do

Grandparents can deal in positive gentleness, while parents must correct because of negative consequences. The very nature of being a parent means they must deal with the things children do wrong. Parents must deal both negatively to correct, and positively to build them up. Paul gave both views when he said, "Father, provoke not your children to wrath [negative], but bring them up in the nurture and admonition [positive] of the Lord" (Eph. 6:4). Both negative and positive influences are needed to bring up a child with a balanced view of life. In a negative sense, the book of Proverbs exhorts, "Correct thy son, and he shall give thee rest" (Prov. 29:17). And in a positive sense, the book of Proverbs said, "Now therefore, listen to me, my children, for blessed are those who keep my ways" (Prov. 8:32).

Good grandparents don't have to deal with a child's disobedience and troubles, unless it directly involves the grandparents. When grandchildren walk through the door of their grandparent's home, a new leaf is turned, and a clear page appears. All the problems a child had at home are forgotten when grandmother cooks for them, or grandpa begins telling stories. Grandparents treat the child with more maturity—forgetting failures—and the child will respond to the positive assessment of their grandparents. Because grandparents think the child is much more grown up than they are—and treat them that way—the child responds by acting grown up.

Grandparents point out your future greatness, while parents must deal with your present shortcomings. The difference here is in focus; grandparents usually have a long-range focus, because they see the big picture of life. Grandparents are exhorted, "A good man leaves an inheritance to his children's children" (Prov. 13:22). Because of grandparents' long look, the Psalmist promises, "Yes, may you see your children's children" (Ps. 128:6). But parents have to deal with their children's disobedience. "Foolishness is bound in the heart of a child; but the rod of correction should drive it far from him"

(Prov. 22:15). Also, parents are exhorted to "withhold not correction of the child" (Prov. 23:13). And what about the permissive parent? "But a child left to himself brings shame to his mother" (Prov. 29:15).

Grandparents can build individual imitative, while parents must teach responsibility and accountability. Basically, both parents are necessary. Grandparents and parents deal in both negative and positive areas, i.e., both deal with the child's rebellion (negative) and both deal with the child's ambition (positive). However, for the most part grandparents can build up a child's initiative because they can focus on the grandchild's assertiveness and inquisitiveness. But parents must focus on accountability: "Children, obey your parents in all things, for this is well pleasing to the Lord" (Col. 3:20). Paul knew that when children were obedient to parents, they would be obedient to all types of authority (political, business, school, church, etc). But at the same time, Paul expressed moderation to the Colossians: "Fathers, do not provoke your children, lest they become discouraged" (Col. 3:21).

Grandparents have learned what is eternally important and what immediately can be overlooked. The Bible speaks continually of a person's "children's children" meaning that grandchildren are our inheritance. Grandparents should rejoice in them, plan for them, leave money to them, and show love to them.

What Is a Disciple-Making Grandparent?

A disciple-making grandparent must be a reproducer of reproducers. A parent can rejoice in a child, as the Bible has said: "Behold, children are a heritage from the LORD" (Ps. 127:3). "Happy is the man who has his quiver full of them [children]" (Ps. 127:5). But, not everyone who has children goes the second mile to correctly rear that child. That's because anyone who has sex can potentially give birth, but it takes something more than sex to be a parent. Sadly, many who have sex outside of marriage are thinking of their own satisfaction. They're not thinking long-range, i.e., they forget that a child can be born out of sexual intercourse. When children are born, there is a responsibility for training and influencing them on this earth, but what about their children, and their children's children? Every child that is born has the potential of producing children like themselves, and grandchildren like themselves. That's why God instituted marriage. The home is a classroom; it's a place where a child is taught principles on how to live. And what parents can't teach, God has given grandparents to energize, motivate, and guide the child to fulfill his/her destiny.

Obviously, most will reproduce themselves physically. But what about reproducing ourselves spiritually, emotionally, socially, and don't forget basic needs, i.e., food, clothing and shelter? Every parent must reproduce themselves in their children. And they have done a good job when their children reproduce themselves in every way in their grandchildren.

The Bible teaches that parents are to pour their life into children, so that children may walk on this earth as parents have walked. The book of Deuteronomy instructs, "These words which I command you today shall be in your heart. You shall teach them diligently to your children, and shall talk of them when you sit in your house, when you walk by the way, when you lie down, and when you rise up" (Deut. 6:6-7). This means child rearing is an all-time responsibility of teaching children to live godly as parents have lived before God.

But what about grandparents? If grandparents pour their life into their children, then their children will live as they live. That's the goal: reproducing grandparents whose children and children's children live as their grandparents. They must love God as the grandparents love God, and serve God as the grandparents served God.

Some parents may try to "beat" a child into submission (obviously, that's not the way to do it), and the child may live outwardly a Christian life, but because they have been beaten into submission, the child has not inwardly taken on the values and attitudes of their parent. As soon as the child gets away from their parents, they become prodigals. The child rejects all that the parent beat into them. However, the goal is for grandchildren to live the way his parents and grandparents taught him: "Children's children are the crown of old men, and the glory of children is their father" (Prov. 17:6).

Disciple-making grandparents will outlive their lessons. The way you live before your children and grandchildren will stretch into the future beyond your life. So, how you treat your children is the way they will treat their children. Hence, the way you treat our children will make you a good grandparent. To become a godly reproducer of godly grandchildren you must produce godliness into your children.

Children are mimickers; they follow examples, and not necessarily what is told them. That means the lessons of childhood are more caught than taught. You can tell your children to love other people and to share their toys, but if they see and feel your selfish attitudes, they won't become a giving person.

Paul told Timothy, four generations is the acid test of child-drearing credibility. Paul (the first generation) poured his life into Timothy (the second generation) who poured his life into faithful men (the third generation); they did the same to others (fourth generation). That means you must pour your life into your children; they in turn must pour that life into your grandchildren. But, your grandchildren are not really reproducers of reproducers until your great-grandchildren live the same way you live. Hence, it takes four generations before you become a reproducer of reproducers.

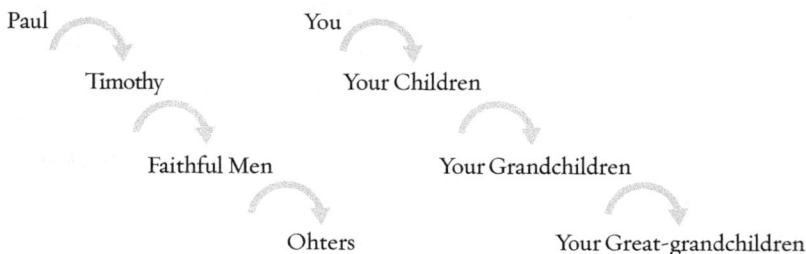

Paul

    Timothy

       Faithful Men

         Ohters

You

    Your Children

       Your Grandchildren

         Your Great-grandchildren

Reproducing grandparents pour their souls into grandchildren. Paul did not just share the Gospel with those he won to Christ. Notice, he poured his total life into new converts: "We were gentle among you, just as a nursing mother cherishes her own children. So, affectionately longing for you, we were well pleased to impart to you not only the gospel of God, but also our own lives, because you had become dear to us" (1 Thess. 2:7-8, author's translation). What does a nursing mother do for her child? She loves . . . she protects . . . she provides . . . she encourages . . . she gives life-giving food. That's what a reproducing grandparent must do for both children and grandchildren.

Disciple-making grandparents become necessary to grandchildren. When you begin to build a foundation into your children or grandchildren, they depend on you for strength and guidance. Just as a foundation gives direction and determines the size of the building, so too reproducing grandparents determine the future of their children and grandchildren. Children do not always understand all that they need to do, nor do they understand how they are to live. They depend upon parents and grandparents for continued direction in their life. Therefore, grandparents have a disciple-making role in their life.

Disciple making is not something you do once and you're finished. Disciple making is not a one-time event; rather, disciple-making is a continuous lifetime activity. You become a disciple-maker in informal times as you talk with them while riding in the car, by example as you read the Scriptures, by counsel as you coach them how to repair something, or as you direct them through complicated relationships with others.

Disciple-making grandparents have not finished until their grandchildren pour into others what they have poured into them. The acid test of a disciple-maker is their disciples. Proverbs says, "The just man walks in his integrity; his children are blessed after him" (Prov. 20:7). And what does that mean? "Children's children are the crown of old men" (Prov. 17:6). The disciple-maker who has good children is described as having fruitful children, i.e., "Your children like olive plants all around your table" (Ps. 128:3). The grandparents who follow the Lord are blessed of Him: "Yes, may you see your children's children" (Ps. 128:6).

What Does a Disciple Look Like?

A disciple of Jesus Christ doesn't look anything like the typical American church member. There are a lot of Christians who are just typical American church members, and maybe many of them will go to Heaven; but their lives do not compare with those who followed Jesus in the First Century.

Too many American church members do not attend church on a regular basis as a statement of their devotion to the Lord. They attend when it's convenient or they give God a little money but they have never approached the level of sacrificial giving. They seldom dig into the Scriptures, nor are they regular prayer intercessors. The typical American church member knows nothing of soul winning, nor investing their lives in ministry. Therefore, if you are a grandparent who wants to disciple your grandchildren, you need to know what a disciple looks like. Before you can become a disciple-maker for your children or grandchildren, you must first become a follower of Jesus Christ.

A disciple makes a radical decision for salvation. A disciple is not just someone who makes a superficial decision to believe in God; they make a radical decision that changes their entire life. Salvation is more than head belief that God exists, and it is more than an emotional stirring of the heart, and it is more than saying yes with one's will. It takes a total life-commitment to Jesus Christ. Salvation involves all three: intellect, emotion, and will; as these three elements of your personality respond positively to the Word of God. But discipleship involves your physical life, your family life, your business life . . . everything! Through the Bible we are saved: "So then faith comes by hearing, and hearing by the word of

God" (Rom. 10:17). Through the Word of God we are born again and receive a new nature: "Of His own will He brought us forth by the word of truth" (Jas. 1:18). Those who respond to His invitation to follow Jesus Christ are actually obeying His words, because as God, Jesus spoke the Word of God: "If anyone desires to come after Me, let him deny himself, and take up his cross daily, and follow Me" (Luke 9:23).

A disciple dedicates himself to be like Jesus. Not only must we make a decision to follow Jesus, as a disciple you must become like Jesus. Peter explains this process, "Christ . . . leaving us an example, that you should follow His steps" (1 Pet. 2:21). Therefore, disciple-making grandparents must live like Jesus, so their grandchildren will follow their example and become like Jesus.

A disciple learns to abide in Christ. Not only must a disciple know and become like Christ, they must learn to daily abide in Christ: "I am the vine, you are the branches. He who abides in Me, and I in him, bears much fruit; for without Me you can do nothing" (John 15:5). And what does the word abide mean? It means to settle down or to remain. So when you abide in Jesus, you settle down in Him and remain there. Your grandchildren need to see your continual relationship to Christ. You must continually talk to them about Jesus. If they don't come to the house of God on a regular basis, they must see you there when they attend.

A disciple obeys and lives by the Scriptures. Those who are disciples have a passion for the Word of God, and have dedicated themselves to live by the Word of God. "If you abide in My word, you are My disciples indeed. And you shall know the truth, and the truth shall make you free" (John 8:31-32). Have your grandchildren seen you make hard decisions to follow Jesus? If yes, good! If no, explain to them how you obey Jesus so they will know you better, and understand your faith better. However, don't live on yesterday's experiences; make Jesus real today. If you are a radical disciple, there'll be tough decisions to make on a continual basis. There is no growth in Christ without change, and there is no change without discarding the old and choosing the new. As you grow daily in the Scriptures, let your grandchildren know what you are learning and how you are growing.

A disciple knows how to pray. It is not enough just to know Christ and to follow Him daily; a disciple must converse with Him each day. You must talk to Him about your needs and desires: "If you abide in Me, and My words abide in you, you will ask what you desire, and it shall be done for you" (John 15:7). The best way to become a disciple-maker of your grandchildren is to pray with them. This can be done at meals, but do more than pray for the food. Find out what's going on in their life, and pray with them about their concerns. When they leave to return home, pray with them about a safe journey, especially if it's a long trip. And don't forget to ask them how you can pray for them while they are away.

A disciple makes Christian love a distinguishing mark of life. A true disciple does not hate, but loves. Sometime it is difficult for children to obey their parents; because all children think they are justified in their disobedience. However, parents must discipline them in love. They must not only teach what is right, they must also teach what is wrong. That way they teach the real meaning of love: "A new commandment I give to you, that you love one another; as I have loved you, that you also love one another" (John 13:34). Your life must be characterized by love if you are going to be a radical disciple of Jesus.

A disciple witnesses to unsaved people and serves others. Those who are disciples will share their faith with lost people, both by being a good testimony, "You shall be witnesses to me" (Acts 1:8), as well as by giving the plan of salvation to them. By serving other people, grandparents demonstrate they are both servants of Jesus Christ, and they follow the example of Christ in their disciple-making role. Grandparents must live as they expect their grandchildren to live: "Greater love has no one than this, than to lay down one's life for his friends" (John 15:13)

How Disciple-making Grandparents Do It

Disciple-making by example. Paul told Timothy, "You have carefully followed my doctrine, manner of life, purpose, faith, longsuffering, love, perseverance, persecutions . . ." (2 Tim. 3:10-11). Timothy knew Paul well. Timothy had heard Paul's sermons, but more importantly, Timothy had seen how Paul responded to opposition. When Paul was physically stoned in Lystra, Timothy saw it all and knew one day he might die a martyr's death. In each and every experience, Timothy learned how to be a disciple of Jesus Christ. As Albert Schweitzer observed, "Example is not the main thing, it is the only thing."[1]

Good parents become disciple-makers by association. That means grandparents must spend time with their grandchildren to influence them for Jesus Christ. And in their relationship, grandparents must demonstrate acceptance, love and a desire for grandchildren to walk with God. Notice how Paul called Timothy "My beloved son" (2 Tim. 1:2). You can almost feel the passion Paul has for Timothy in his introduction to this letter. Do your grandchildren feel they are "your beloved sons and daughters"?

Grandparents become disciple-makers by assignment. Paul did not want to just tell Timothy lessons or doctrine; rather, he put young Timothy to work serving the Lord. Paul sent Timothy to minister in Corinth, Macedonia, Philippi, Thessalonica, etc. When Paul was run out of Thessalonica by a mob that wanted to kill him, Paul left Timothy to preach the Gospel and build up the church. When Paul was in prison in Rome, Timothy was sent to Ephesus to pastor the church in that city. Paul was not afraid to give young Timothy a difficult assignment, probably not just to train Timothy, but to get the work of Christ done. In the same way, you have to give your grandchildren assignments. Can you bribe them to learn Scripture verses by offering a baked apple pie or whatever they want? Can you financially help them on a student missionary trip to Appalachia or Central America? Can you think of other assignments where your grandchildren could grow in Christ?

Grandparents become disciple-makers by instruction. How did Paul disciple Timothy? Probably through the content of his preaching and teaching. Timothy heard Paul preach publicly and privately, and he learned what discipleship meant in the process. Timothy was not just another face in the crowd. Paul reminded Timothy to pass on the message, "you heard of me" (2 Tim. 2:2). Grandparents will need to take the time and energy to instruct—systematically— the things their grandchildren need to know. Remember, some of the greatest lessons are taught in 10 seconds by the "minute-teacher." You can change lives quickly when your lesson meets the desperate need that your grandchild seeks. Also, some lessons may take a lifetime to communicate. Whatever it takes, be ready to do it.

Grandparents become disciple-makers by private counsel. There were probably many intimate conversations between Paul and Timothy that were not written down because they were private. However, we do have their personal correspondence. Paul wrote to Timothy in two letters instructing him about his medical problems (1 Tim. 5:23), telling him not to be bashful and reluctant (1 Tim. 4:12), telling him to stir up his gift (2 Tim. 1:6), telling him to handle older elders in the church (1 Tim. 5:1), telling him how to handle widows and children (1 Tim. 5:3-7), and a number of other personal items. You'll want to counsel your grandchildren when they bring problems to you, and sometimes you'll have to tenderly approach them when they have a problem but are reluctant to approach you. Counsel them! Counseling is problem solving, counseling is decision-making, counseling is pointing them toward the future.

Grandparents become disciple-makers by encouragement. Notice, Paul was not reluctant to encourage young Timothy. First he listed Timothy's name with his names six times in the Word of God. This is encouragement by association. Then, Paul publicly expressed appreciation for Timothy (1 Tim. 4:17) and told the Philippians, "For I have no one like-minded [like Timothy] who will sincerely care for your state" (Phil. 2:20). So, what does that mean for grandparents? It's all right to brag about grandchildren, because that's one way of encouraging them, i.e., reinforcing their discipleship to Jesus Christ. When a grandparent tells someone about how their grandchildren follow the Lord—in front of their grandchildren—it may motivate the grandchildren to live up to the expectations of their grandparents.

Grandparents become disciple-makers by prodding. Timothy was reluctant and at times bashful. Timothy probably needed a jump start for his ministry. So, Paul told him, "Stir up the gift of God which is in you" (2 Tim. 1:6). Again, he told him, "Be strong" (2 Tim. 2:1), warning him not to give heed to "deceiving spirits and doctrines of demons" (1 Tim. 4:1), and "Neglect not the gift that is in you" (1 Tim. 4:14). What does that mean for grandparents? Sometimes you will have to prod your grandchildren into Christian service. This doesn't always mean scolding; it can be an innocent question: "How did you like church?" (That's a sly way of finding out if they went to church.) You could ask, "What did you get out of Bible study?" (which is a sly way of finding out if they are reading the Scriptures). Also, you could ask, "What is the greatest thing you are praying for? (That's a sly way of finding out if they are praying and trusting God for things in their life.) Finally, you can ask, "How can I pray for you?"

Note
1. Albert Schweitzer "Example Is Not The Main Thing" (quote), http://www.brainy-quote.com/quotes/quotes/a/q112973.html (3 March 2003).

Reading Bibliography

A Grandparent's Gift of Love: True Stories of Comfort, Hope and Wisdom by Edward Fays, New York: Warner Books, Inc., September 2002. Stories and lessons learned from his grandparents offer hope and comfort.

Contemporary Grandparenting by Arthur Kornhaber, London: SAGE Publications, January 1996. Synthesizes the current knowledge about grandparents' identity, the drive to grandparent, and grandparents' roles in the family and society. Offers a contemporary and perceptive view for grandparents who desire to know their role in depth, and also for professionals who deal with grandparent-related issues: teachers, therapists, attorneys, judges, and governmental workers.

God's Greatest Gift—Grandparents by Sheila R. Davidson, Baltimore: American Literary Press, Inc.; January 2002. This is a lovely book of poetry by young children extolling their love for, and the varied virtues of their grandparents.

Grand-Stories: 101+ Bridges of Love Joining Grandparents & Grandkids by Ernie Wendell, Pleasanton, TX: Friendly Oaks Publications, March 2000. Honors the grandparent-grandchild relationship and the powerful bond between them.

Grandloving. Making Memories With Your Grandchildren by Sue Johnson and Julie Carlson, Fairport, NY: Heartstrings Press, 3rd edition, February 2003. This is an upbeat, easy-to-read sourcebook on how grandparents can have fun and make memories with their grandchildren.

Grandma, I Need Your Prayers: Blessing Your Grandchildren Through the Power of Prayer by Quin Sherrer and Ruthanne Garlock, Grand Rapids: Zondervan Publishing Company, February 2002. Written by two grandmothers, this book uses stories that testify to the remarkable power of prayer, along with Scriptures and prayers readers can use with their children.

Grandpa Told Me. . . Things Your Father Meant to Tell You by Joe Baker, Irvine, CA: Joe Baker & Associates. A creative book full of wisdom and down-to-earth, relevant advice "not just to my grandsons, but also to those of you who did not get a chance to know your own grandfathers, and to those who knew their grandfathers but are not real sure of just what it was their grandfathers told them or were trying to tell them." There are sections giving advice on money, education, clothes, recreation, possessions and lots more.

Grandparent Power: How to Strengthen the Vital Connection Among Grandparents, Parents, and Children by Arthur Kornhaber, New York: Random House Value Publishing, Inc., August 1995. Offers advice on how to connect grandparents with their grandchildren and provides them with concrete solutions for overcoming the problems that arise from grandparenting in the 1990s.

Grandparenting: It's Not What It Used to Be: Expert Answers to the Questions Grandparents Ask Most by Irene Endicott, Nashville: Broadman & Holman Publishers, April 1997. Answers questions from men and women concerned with their rights and responsibilities as grandparents, offering a unique blend of practical advice and Christian nurturing.

Grandparenting by Grace: A Guide Through the Joys and Struggles by Irene Endicott, Nashville: Broadman & Holman Publishers, October 1994.

Commentary based on personal experiences and interviews of grandparents. This covers interesting suggestions and advice on how to deal with single parenting in the 1990s.

Grandparents/Grandchildren—The Vital Connection by Arthur Kornhaber, Somerset, NJ: Transaction Publishers, October 1991. Explores the unique emotional attachments between grandparents and grandchildren. It also explores the loss of those attachments and the effects of that loss on children, older people and society.

Grandparents as Parents: A Survival Guide for Raising a Second Family by Sylvie de Toledo and Deborah Edler Brown, New York: Guilford Publications, July 1995. A resource book for grandparents raising their grandchildren with helpful hints concerning getting through the red tape, support groups, and other aspects of this complex and rewarding experience.

Heart to Heart: Stories for Grandparents by Joe Wheeler, Wheaton: Tyndale House Publishers, September 2002. Abounds with life lessons, celebrates memories of grandfather and grandmother, and is a treasure-chest of stories that teaches timeless truths about the relationship between grandparents and their grandchildren.

Learning from Little Ones, "Tales from a Grandfather's Heart" by Gilman Smith, Frisco, CO: Papaco Press, April 2000. Contains lovely and inspiring stories about gifts that children give their grandparents.

Living the Lois Legacy: Passing on a Lasting Faith to Your Grandchildren by Helen Hosier, Wheaton: Tyndale House Publishers, September 2002. Contains stories of grandparents giving their grandchildren the roots of faith that will sustain them through their lives.

Second Time Around by Joan Callander, Baton Rouge: Bookpartners, March 2000. This is a new book for grandparents raising grandchildren, based on the author's personal and professional experience.

The Essential Grandparent: A Guide for Making a Difference by Lillian Carson, Edison, NJ: Health Communications, Inc., May 1996. Honors grandparenthood, dispels grandparenting myths and helps readers develop their own grandparenting strategy in order to make the most of this rewarding stage in life.

That's What Grandfathers Are For by Arlene Uslander, Chicago: Chicago Spectrum Press,1996. A book of poetry that touches the core of what happens between grandparents and grandchildren. This poem speaks for the book: "I had an old, old fiddle from when I was a boy, and when I'd play a tune or two, your face lit up with joy. You clapped your hands and stamped your feet; we had a good old time. And if I played some sour notes...you never seemed to mind. No sooner did I play one song, then you'd say, 'Papa, more!' So I'd raise my bow and tap my toe, (That's what grandfathers are for.)"

That's What Grandparents Are For by Arlene Uslander, Gilsum, NH: Peel Productions; (December 2001). This book celebrates the bond between grandchildren and grandparents.

The 12 Rules of Grandparenting by Susan Kettman, New York: Checkmark Books, November 1999. Contains straightforward advice on developing a positive attitude, baby-sitting, fun projects, dealing with grandchildren, dealing with family issues and more.

The ABCs of Christian Grandparenting by Robert G. Bruce and Debra Bruce, St. Louis: Concordia Publishing House, February 1999.

The Gift of Grandparenting: Building Meaningful Relationships with Your Grandchildren by Eric E. Wiggin and Gary D. Chapman, Wheaton: Tyndale House Publishers, July 2001. Encourages grandparents to take an active role in creating strong spiritual and emotional family ties. Whether the grandchildren live around the corner or around the country, this book gives every grandparent new ways to enjoy the marvelous gift of grandparenting.

The Grandparent Guide: The Definitive Guide to Coping with the Challenges of Modern Grandparenting by Arthur Kornhaber, Chicago: McGraw-Hill/Contemporary Books, June 2002. Contains over 50 topics relating to grandparents, grandchildren, and parents. For example, raising grandchildren, grandparent development, legal issues, step-grandparenting, family diversity, and more.

The Grandparents Treasure Chest by Edward Fays, New York: Warner Books, Inc., August 2002. This is a keepsake journal that gives grandparents the tool to record their thoughts on being a grandparent.

The Joy of Grandma's Cooking: A Treasury of Recipes and Stories from the Heart by Clarice Carlson Orr, Lincoln, NE: Dageforde Publishing, Inc., September 1999. This book is a collection of some two hundred recipes, most of which are accompanied by short stories.

To Grandma's House We . . . Stay by Sally Houtman, Northridge, CA: Studio 4 Productions, March 1999. Guides grandparents through the turbulent waters of grandparenting their grandchildren, and acting as surrogate parents too!

www.ingramcontent.com/pod-product-compliance
Lightning Source LLC
Chambersburg PA
CBHW060752100426
42813CB00004B/789